POTENTIALIZED

Wake Up! YOU are the Answer!

BRADLEY THOMASON

POTENTIALIZED LLC
MADISON, WI

Potentialized LLC
Website: Potentialized.com
Phone: (608) 514-1850

Ordering Information:
Special discounts are available on quantity purchases by corporations, associations, and others. For details, contact bulkorders@potentialized.com.

Potentialized / Thomason, Bradley. —1st edition
ISBN 978-0-9974280-0-1 (paperback)
ISBN 978-0-9974280-1-8 (ebook)

Library of Congress Control Number: 2016936466

THIS BOOK IS DEDICATED TO THE SPARK
OF THE UNIVERSE RESIDING IN EACH OF US
THAT IS SEEKING FULL EXPRESSION THROUGH US,
AS US, FOR US, AND FOR THE BENEFIT OF ALL.

CONTENTS

CONTENTS

Born naked and vulnerable, dependent and newly separated
Born to explore and contribute to OUR knowing
Born into sublime perfection, the seed for a new world.

We agree to the path of our intertwined awakening
We agree to hurt and be hurt, to love and be loved,
to seek and be sought
We agree to be broken so that we will find our way back to wholeness.

Confused, lost, alone, and grieving
for something only faintly remembered.
Driven forward by complex pain—the fuel for our awakening.
Smiling through sad eyes and loving through broken hearts, we long
to know the beauty of something lost.

WE watch and celebrate your struggle with jealous patience.
WE long to play with you in the sandbox of emotion
and the duality of matter.
WE are always here, willing co-conspirators at your beckoning.
Loving you with pure hearts.

Born the blueprint for, and master of Y(OUR) creation.
Born to become, you do so beautifully.
Born pure potential, waiting for you to believe.

Believe!

CHAPTER ONE

POTENTIALIZED

The wisdom and means to potentialize
are alive within all things.

The path to deep fulfillment, to the realization of our potential, is designed by the Universe to be one of ease. A process of gentle becoming. Of steady and purposeful movement toward the highest and best version of ourselves.

It is not possible to be purposeless. Purpose is embedded in all things by design. A thing is always created with a unique purpose and the means to achieve it. An acorn contains all the instructions to create the mighty oak. Within the caterpillar are all the instructions on how to transform into a butterfly. Everywhere in nature this is true.

Given this, why do we humans struggle to know our purpose and realize our potential? Are we the only exceptions to this rule in an otherwise perfectly designed universe? I think not. I would argue that each of us is born with a purpose and the natural ability to achieve that purpose. Each of us is part of a grand plan. Each of us is a perfectly designed organism within a perfectly designed system. That is the order of things.

Any struggle is our own. An acorn does not struggle to become the oak tree. A caterpillar does not struggle to become a butterfly. A flower does not struggle to bloom. A fawn does not struggle to run within hours of its birth or to grow into a full-grown deer. They simply allow their own becoming as it was designed by a benevolent universe without resistance or judgment. The absence of struggle could be our reality, our truth, too, if we would only get out of the way by remembering

1

who we truly are and why we are here—and then surrendering to our own becoming.

We humans are the only creatures on this extraordinary planet that struggle AGAINST our own becoming. We fight the innate wisdom that is always seeking to realize the highest within us. Perhaps by design, we have forgotten who we are and why we are here, and so we struggle to rediscover and remember the unique spark of the universe seeking expression through us. Remembering and rediscovering cannot be done through the mind, they can only be done by letting go and allowing our true nature to express unobstructed through our being and our human instrument—our whole mind-body-soul organism.

Why do we struggle against our birthright? Why do we struggle against being and becoming who and what we were created to be? As I watched everything around me in nature *become* with such ease, face death and loss without mourning, and live fully in each moment, I asked the Universe the questions: Why do I struggle? Why do WE struggle?

The Universe responded: "Your struggles lie within your mind. They are not real, but they become real to you when you create them through thoughts, words, and actions as experiences, and respond with emotion and make them real."

Nearly ALL of our struggles are of the mind. We ate of the proverbial apple from the Tree of Knowledge, and ever since then our minds have ripped us from being and landed us in a world plagued by excessive thought and analysis. Our knowing moved from the body and heart into the mind and we lost our connection to that from which we came—nature—and from the all-knowing, benevolent Universe where all our answers, experiences, and wisdom are held. Specifically, we lost the wisdom of who we are and why we are here and the innate ability to expand into our unique potential and truest expression in this and every lifetime.

Potentialized is the state of having realized our potential. It is both a dynamic and fixed state of being. In any given moment, it is true that we are potentialized—even when we struggle. Who we are, what we are, and where we are in our lives represents the very best of us in that moment. We may judge our bests to be less than what we want to be (or think we could or should be), but it is the very best we can do simply because it already is what is.

If we could have done better, we would have.

If we could have done differently, we would have.

The best part of being potentialized is that the Universe is overjoyed by whatever we have achieved and created. It celebrates every thought we think, every word we speak, and every action we take without exception. It does not judge anything we do as good or bad, right or wrong. The Universe has no desire for us other than that which we desire for ourselves. The Universe just enthusiastically says, "YES, I will help you create whatever you want." And it does. It conspires on our behalf in every moment, loving us, supporting us, helping us, and guiding us.

Again, we need only look to the natural world to see the truth of this. If what happens on Earth is evidence of its dynamics, then our benevolent Universe does not revere birth over death. Both are fundamental to the functioning of Earth's ecosystem. Everything is food for something else—whether an animal, a plant, an insect, a bacterium, or a virus. All living creatures express: We breathe, sing, dance, eat, poop, fight, kill, and love—and the Universe smiles because it is all by design. All perfect, however it is.

Judgment of good vs. bad is a human invention. It is not a trait of the Creator. If it was a trait of the Creator, then the rules of beliefs like religion would be objectively applied to all living things within creation and not just to our single species. We have created judgment and imprisoned ourselves within it. We are our own jailers. If we choose to believe another's judgment of us, we step into the prison of that judgment, close the door, and turn the key. When we choose to believe our mind's judgment of us we allow it to imprison us.

Judgment is taught. How do I know this? Because judgments of right vs. wrong vary widely by culture, society, family, and religion. Depending on the circumstances into which you were born, your beliefs and the resulting judgments will be different.

Judgment, dear brothers and sisters, is the greatest force inhibiting our potential. Every moment we are choosing what we create and the Universe is celebrating and supporting our choices. Every choice and the resulting experiences are perfect if there is no judgment.

If we want more sadness, the Universe will help us create more sadness. If we want more joy, the Universe will help us create more joy. If we want more suffering, the Universe will help us create more suffering. We tend to identify with the illusion of the dense 3D playground we live in and with the programming that our experiences in life install in our minds. But the Universe knows that within our being is the knowing that *we ourselves are the Universe.* We are Creators endowed with the same power of creation that created the heavens and the Earth. We are Creators at the leading edge of creation, simultaneously experiencing and adding to creation. We cannot "get it wrong" because everything we think, say, and do adds to our understanding of creation. Every moment is a new moment, a blank canvas on which to create the next moment, so in every moment we have a choice as to what we create and who we create ourselves to be through those choices.

Don't believe me? Test it out. Stop whatever it is you are doing and whatever it is you are thinking in this moment.

If you need to, say the word *STOP,* either by whispering it or by shouting it to disrupt the moment, and then repeat it until you find an empty moment where the mind is silent.

Pause in the silence of no thought, word, or action. Feel the potential.

You can do ANYTHING next. You can think any thought, speak any word, or take any action you desire. So what do you choose? More of what got you to where you are? Or something new, different?

Are you going to let fear or love govern your next choice? Those are really the only two choices we have, EVER. Fear vs. love is the duality behind all thoughts, words, and deeds, the duality behind all choices.

Look around at your life now, in every detail, and see what

you have created one thought, word, and deed at a time. Look at your relationships, your health, your profession, your family, your finances, and your home. What you see and experience is the cumulative result of years of creating through thinking, speaking, and doing—one thought stacked upon another, one word spoken after another, one action performed after another.

Whatever your creation, know this: You are loved and celebrated for it because it is the very best you could do and it is MAGNIFICENT.

I applaud you for the beauty and ugliness of your creation. For the perfect imperfection of it. It is a masterpiece in the making, a masterpiece you will continue perfecting until you take your last breath.

Most importantly, in the moment of no thought, word, or action into which you have entered, YOU ARE AWAKENED to what you have created and aware of the opportunity the next moment represents. Bask in this moment. In the in-between. It is a field of pure potentiality. Here you are both potentialized and potentializing simultaneously. The only difference about this moment is that for the moment you have awakened into a state of conscious awareness about being potentialized. Whether you remain awakened in the next moment is your choice.

I know what you are probably experiencing in this moment because I know what I experienced when I woke up to my role as creator in my creation: terror, sadness, depression, elation, hope, anger, joy, excitement, and more. When I woke up to my creation I thought, *How could this possibly be my best? How could I be totally and utterly responsible for THIS?!* At the same time, I knew that it was true, and I was overwhelmed by this truth. As I examined this revelation more deeply, everywhere I looked I saw evidence that the choice was mine to think every thought, speak every word, and perform every action that got me to where I was.

There is always a choice point at every thought, word, and action. ALWAYS. These are like the forks in the road of our creative process. Although to most of us it feels as if our thoughts and words and actions have chosen us, we choose what comes next. We have always had a choice. In some moments we are overwhelmed by emotions like fear or anger or anxiety or excitement or joy, but underneath there is always a choice. If we only had the awareness and mastery to slow down the moment, calm the emotion, and see the fork in the road so that we could have chosen consciously, we might have chosen differently, but we have done the best we could. That best was perfect simply because it was.

I discovered the truth about the choice we have in every moment one day while doing one of my favorite hikes on Cold Springs Trail in Santa Barbara, California. I started the hike feeling light and happy. I was there in the beauty of nature with my dog, Brooks, and it was perfect. Until it wasn't. In a matter of moments, I went from being carefree and happy to being depressed.

It must have been the extreme contrast of juxtaposing these states that made me pause and ask HOW? And WHY? And thank the Universe (*you're welcome*) that I did. For in this moment of pausing to step back, I was able to trace the shift in my state of being back to a single thought. A single thought that said, *You're a failure, Bradley. What are you doing with your life?* The real trouble began when I believed the thought because that thought then lead to another and another, and suddenly, listed out in my mind were all the reasons why the first thought was true.

Then my emotions responded to these thoughts.

My emotional state spiraled into negativity and heaviness and depression and sadness. But the truth was that nothing had changed in my outward life. I was still Bradley Thomason hiking on his favorite trail in Santa Barbara. That was the only thing that was objectively true. All the rest of my experience was the creation of my mind, a creation that I chose to believe and respond to.

This experience of spinning into a challenging emotion state, or *negative thought spiral,* awakened me to the fork in the road that exists in every moment. It proved to me the ability I have to choose my thoughts AND to believe or disbelieve them.

Once I realized what had happened, I decided to attempt

a countermeasure to spiral me back to the place I had started. So I shouted, "STOP!" Then I said, "Mind, I will no longer allow you to beat me up and make me feel small and worthless. I love you and I know you are not by nature judgmental, you are not by nature a bully, so I am asking you to stop. Let us work together to create more positivity and self-acceptance within so we can start to mirror the same outside us."

After this, I verbally interjected all the authentic positivity I could access. I told myself, "I am beautiful and brave. I have chosen to leave a life that did not make me happy and venture forth into the unknown, and it is scary. And I know, mind, that you are scared for me, but we can do this, we are smart and capable and extraordinary, and this time is simply a bridge to a new life that we will discover as we put one foot in front of the other." As I did this, I felt my mood shift. I felt my emotions lighten, and hope and joy returned. I also realized that I was at war with a mind that had internalized external judgments such that it had become the judger when no one else was there to do it. WOW, I thought, *Why would anyone do this to themselves?*

In that moment, I expressed my gratitude for having momentarily awakened to my power as Creator and I vowed to do my best to remain awake and choose consciously from then on. And when I couldn't or wouldn't, I would stop the madness of the negative thought spiral by yelling, "STOP," finding space in the field of potentiality, and then choosing to think and believe what was really true about me: that I am radiant and special and beautiful and smart and courageous simply because I AM.

Of course, even after having this cathartic moment, I continued to be hijacked by my mind, but I did have a new tool to counter negative thought spirals, and I used it. In fact, no more than a few hours later, I was again being thrashed around by the powerful negative thoughts of a mind that seemed bent on my destruction. And I responded perfectly to those thoughts with emotions that seemingly dictated the nature of my response through the quality of the words that I spoke and the actions that I took. Through this thought/word/action creative mechanism, I RECREATED more of what I did not want: more depression, more anxiety, more fear, more suffering.

Later, I woke up again and chose better thoughts and actions. Then I went to sleep. Then woke up. And slept. And woke. And so on.

The good news is that the next moment is always a brand-new opportunity to create whatever you want. Instead of going left, you could go right. Instead of saying no, you could say yes. Instead of saying, "Oh, OK," you could say, "Oh, hell no, not this again!" So stop, celebrate your creation, take full and complete responsibility for it, and forgive whomever it is that you've been blaming for your unhappiness, brokenness, or failures (including yourself). Choose instead to discover the singular extraordinary purpose that lies within you that is in cahoots with the Universe to reach its full expression.

Let go of the struggle. When you do, you will realize that you are being carried along by a gentle current that has always been there, pushing you toward the experiences you need to heal and remember and become. Take a deep breath and relax into the flow of this current.

You are as the caterpillar or the acorn. You hold within you all that you need to fully realize a potential unlike any other in the Universe. Your soul, humanity, the Earth, and the Universe itself desire only one thing: the full expression of the extraordinary, miraculous being that is YOU.

You cannot get it wrong. You cannot fail. You will never be judged. You are being celebrated in each moment for what you are able to be and become just because IT IS!

Then, in the very next moment, you have infinite opportunities to choose again and change the trajectory and substance of your creation.

You are a potentialized, potentializing potentializer.

That's what we're here to discuss.

CHAPTER TWO

THE ME I WAS CREATED TO BE

*Wherever you are, whenever you are,
however you are, whatever you are, whoever you are,
there YOU are!*

remember knowing the authentic ME when I was six or seven. The ME I was created to be. I've always remembered this version of myself because I remember that I KNEW with all my being that I was special and extraordinary. At times I even thought I was a holy being come again to the Earth. Now I realize we all are. As a kid, I was confident and smart and inquisitive and social. I engaged with people and the world without fear. I questioned and conversed and explored with glee. I was kind, ALWAYS. I didn't know judgment, as I had never experienced it, and so my authentic self was unobstructed and shone through everything I did and said, and my singularly perfect note and spark danced and expressed and played freely in the world.

I've never lost this memory of ME, this center of my being, this knowing. It was always the place and the version of ME that I longed to return to. It was my North Star through all my searching and suffering and struggling and yearning and awakening and failing and succeeding, appearing as a faint shimmering of light or a soft whisper beckoning me back to ME.

Many times I prayed to be like the boy I was—that version of myself: untainted, unobstructed, and unapologetically ME. The ME before life became painful and confusing and sad, which it did. The ME before my experiences taught me that life was not safe, and that the extraordinary special ME that I loved so much and who was unique in all the world was not enough to be simply accepted and appreciated by other humans, and before expressing myself fully resulted in judgment and pain and condemnation and separation.

There was so much pain. SO, SO MUCH PAIN. At one point I remember the young boy in me saying to myself, *This is not OK. Why is this happening? Doesn't the world know how beautiful and special I am? Why would it treat me like this? Why would it hurt me like this?* Then I made a decision to punish my fellow humans and the world, and the Universe, by taking away the one thing I had to give: ME.

Strangely, I actually remember making this decision.

I was roughly eleven years old.

After that, I took away ME from the world and made it my goal to learn to live in this strange world and to survive in such a way that I would be accepted and could avoid pain and rejection and abandonment. I locked away ME and started to observe what was praised and approved of and I did that. I got good grades. I molded my behavior to be like the other boys my age. I acted more masculine. I got more male friends and fewer female friends. I played more sports. I acted tougher. I went from bullied to bully. I changed the clothes I wore and the way I talked. I also monitored my behavior and made sure I was being appropriate at all times. Fitting in and being liked became my primary goals.

And it worked. Within two years, my life had changed. But the ME I hid inside was sad, which meant I was sad all the time. And I was angry that I couldn't just be myself and instead had to expend so much energy and time trying so hard to be what others wanted me to be. Slowly, day by day, month by month, year by year, as I became less ME and more as I thought the world wanted me to be, the pain grew.

Sadly, it is very easy to tell what the world wants you to be because when you are it, then your friends, family, society, and coworkers approve and praise you. When you are not being it, they judge and condemn and tease you.

As a preteen and teenager, I chose to mold myself into

being, doing, and saying what brought me more acceptance and praise, and in doing so abandoned myself. And while my life became livable in some ways, I was horribly unhappy. I was deeply sad and very angry. Sadness and anger were always underneath and behind my smile. ALWAYS. I wore the mask of a happy boy, when inside nothing could have been further from the truth. Until, when I was nineteen years old, I just couldn't take it one more day. I couldn't play the games or try so hard to fit in and be liked anymore. I was exhausted and miserable and had lost my will to live. And so I quit my regular life, which at the time was consumed by college and my fraternity, and went home, where I had to manufacture an acceptable explanation for being a quitter.

Mind you, this was not a conscious decision, it was a deeper decision. Something deep within me could no longer function as the false self I had created myself to be, which meant I could not function in reality anymore. My ability to play the game failed me and I collapsed in on myself. I felt like I was losing my mind, I felt fractured, I could no longer smile to hide the sadness and anger, and it seemed as if all I could do was cry.

I felt so broken, so far from ME that I didn't care about anything anymore. I couldn't care. I didn't have it in me because I had no more ME to give away. I had so conformed and molded and contorted myself to fit in and please everyone outside myself that I had lost ME. I had abandoned ME. And I didn't even know that this was what I had done. I only know this now, looking back. I just knew that I was in hell. I knew I was lost. I knew that life had lost its sparkle and I had lost my will to live.

Living back at home after dropping out of college, I was miserable. I cried every day. I was depressed and broken. I felt contorted beyond recognition. My whole being was an ugly cry. I was so smart and yet I couldn't figure out WHY this was all happening. Why was I so unhappy? What had happened? How would I fix it? What could I do? I had done what everyone told me would make me happy. I had loved the right people and succeeded in school and then I went to college and joined a fraternity, and I was liked and appreciated for whom I pretended to be. Yet I felt like there was a black hole where my heart used to be. I could make no sense of it.

Today I know that I was so caught up in the web of a falsely woven self that I actually believed I was the man I created myself to be. I wasn't the authentic ME. In actuality, I had created a version of myself that was someone I thought other people wanted me to be, and the tension and disparity between ME and me was creating intolerable suffering. The ME buried deep within literally would not let it go on for even one more day. *Enough,* it cried. *ENOUGH!* It would not allow itself to be turned even one more degree away from itself.

So there I was, back home and suffering in the disparity between me and ME, and still totally unaware that I was the cause of my own suffering. But I could feel the disparity and it was dark.

I was driving around one day thinking, *I have to do something to end the pain.* I couldn't take it anymore. It was too much, too big. So I sat with the choice of ending my life. I imagined what the experience would be like, and I came to know that I held the power to end my own suffering once and for all. In seeing this, I also recognized that if I did end my life, there was no coming back. It would be final. Like, final final. Not just sort of, or temporarily final. And in that moment of recognition that spark within me that was always there, the spark of ME in me called out.

It really must have been one hell of a cry, because I heard it even through the darkness and despair of my suffering.

The image that comes to mind is the moment in the Dr. Seuss storybook *Horton Hears a Who* when the speck that is the entire world of the Whos that lives on a single flower that Horton holds in his trunk are about to be lowered into hot oil. Horton is roped and tied and has lost the struggle to convince others that he isn't crazy and that there really is a world of tiny beings living on a speck on the flower he is holding, when at last all the little Whos living on the speck pull together and they shout and sing out, "HELLO," and finally they are heard.

That's what it was like. The ME that was buried deeply inside me sang out and finally broke through after all the years of trying, and whatever it was that I heard, it was enough for me to consider another path.

The inspiration emerged that I could figure out the WHY of my unhappiness . . . and if I figured it out, I could live a different and happier life . . . and I could find the joy and fuller expression of who I faintly remembered myself to be. That's how I chose to walk a different path instead: the long, winding, challenging path of remembering and discovering and unlearning and deprogramming what had gotten me—a human boy of nineteen years of age named Bradley, who lived on a speck of dust in an infinite Universe called Earth—to such a dark and miserable place.

Like Horton and the Whos, once ME broke through and I could hear it, it had plenty to say. And the first thing it said was, "Let's get outta here. Let's leave behind this reality that is causing you so much pain, and give you a break and a chance to become reacquainted with YOU. You need a break from the reality molded by your family and friends and society and culture and socioeconomics and race and politics and religion and sexuality." And so a destination emerged from inside and I bought a ticket and packed a backpack and left.

I just left.

Something made me trust ME enough to do the scary and unthinkable: to leap into the void of not knowing.

I had nothing to lose at this point anyway, right? So I leapt.

I had never done anything like that before. Who was I? And now what? I hadn't thought that far ahead. But it was a good thing I hadn't, because if I had THOUGHT it through with the mind that had created it all in the first place, I wouldn't have done it.

In the weeks that followed my departure from my childhood home, I found ME without even knowing what it was that I had found. The ME that had been smothered by shoulds and that I had contorted in order to achieve others' acceptance and avoid others' rejection got to reemerge. And I remembered ME and felt joy again. I smiled authentically for what seemed like the first time in years.

Each day I got up and did what I wanted and expressed the ME I remembered myself to be, and it felt good. SOOOOOO very good. Deep down to ME good.

It would take me many years to realize that in working so hard to avoid the pain of judgment and rejection and abandonment, I had created an even deeper pain: the pain of judging and rejecting and abandoning the ME the Universe created me to be. I internalized the external judgment and fueled by this now self-judgment I left ME behind. The ME I was at six that shone so brightly and who was always there deep inside, unceasingly, though faintly, calling me back to ME. I had locked ME away to punish the world for the pain of living, but the only one I had ended up punishing was myself.

For nearly thirty years following that discovery, I searched and read more books than I care to admit. I attended many seminars and went on many spiritual retreats in my quest to find one piece of knowing (or the key or the answer or the learning) that would bring me lasting happiness and fulfillment instead of just fleeting experiences of them. What was it that would help get me to the place I was obsessively searching for? Was it the perfect job? Was it caring for the Earth? Was it the perfect love? Was it the perfect orgasm? Was it enlightenment? Was it ascension? Was it awakening? Was it money? Was it having my chakras balanced or my aura repaired? Was it in forgiveness? Was it gratitude? I tried everything I could think of, and still I searched.

Over those three decades, I would experience periods of relief from struggle, periods of happiness and balance, but they never lasted long and so my searching continued. Until one day, during one particular experience, the Universe spoke to me and said, "ENOUGH! Stop searching. Stop trying to fix anyone or anything. Stop trying to save the Earth. Stop trying to fix your relationships. Stop trying to find the perfect job or lover or friendship. Stop trying so very hard to make money. Stop trying to be better, do better, think better, love better, know better, feel better, give better, or pray better.

"Stop trying to shine brighter. Stop looking 'out there' for the answers. There is only one thing for you to do. There has only ever been one thing for you to do. BE YOU. Be the YOU I created you to be. You are like a snowflake, a perfect and unique expression of me, and the only one in all my creation. Yet you spend all your time and energy searching for something you cannot possibly find out there anywhere because YOU are it. You are the answer. Allow YOU to be. Allow YOU to shine. Allow YOU to become.

"You left YOU, but YOU never left you. Only when you stop searching can you realize and come home to this simple, yet profound truth.

"I created you to be YOU. Just like I created that eagle to be that eagle, and that hippopotamus to be that hippopotamus, and that bacterium to be that bacterium, and that platypus to be that platypus, and that cloud to be that cloud, and that oak tree to be that oak tree, and that spider to be that spider, and that molecule to be that molecule. I created you to be YOU. Stop getting in your own way and overthinking everything.

"Being YOU is simple. Breathe in, there YOU are. Breathe out, there YOU are. Drive to whatever job you have and there YOU are. Whatever relationships you are in, there YOU are again. YOU are wherever you are, whenever you are, however you are, whatever you are, whoever you are. There YOU are.

"Being YOU does not require a thing to change. It only requires you to remember and recognize the ME in YOU. YOU are perfect. I don't make mistakes. YOU are perfect right here and right now simply because YOU ARE!

"Stop praying for change or for things to be different, and awaken to YOU right NOW! And help others do the same, help others be the perfect, singular expressions of ME that they can be! Stop judging. Listen to me: STOP JUDGING. Stop judging yourself, stop judging others, just STOP! It is what keeps you trapped and what keeps others trapped. You all are imprisoned by judgments. Start loving every expression of ME. Everyone is different, so get used to it. Stop arguing about who's right, 'cause you know what? No one is RIGHT and you're all RIGHT. There, that's solves that.

"Every human being has only one thing to do in this lifetime: As this gift I created YOU to be, engaged in this dance of Spirit with matter, you are to be YOU, fully, brightly, unapologetically, radiantly.

"Sing your singular note loudly and proudly into the symphony of creation. Allow the unique frequency that YOU are to simply BE. That is enough. YOU are enough! YOU are the one you've been searching for! YOU are the answer!"

This communication was so profound—so deep, so simple, so true—that eventually it pushed me to write this book. As I did so, I realized that I now stand at the end of a journey of some forty-eight years of living and simultaneously at the beginning of a new journey that, at a minimum, will certainly take me to the other side of this moment. *Phew,* it did.

Hopefully, Universe willing, this journey will last some number of days, weeks, months, and years into an unknown and uncertain future.

These days I do not pretend to be an expert on anything but ME, and even that I'm still perfecting. I'd say I used to think I was an expert on many things in my impetuous youth, but the wiser me now knows that I am a novice at best. I have no degree in psychology, religious studies, or physics (quantum or otherwise) that would particularly qualify me to write a book about how the Universe designed humanity to be potentialized. My university has been life. I have a degree in being human because I am human. And while I know that I will never master being human (because as long as I draw breath there will be more to learn and remember and awaken to), I have arrived at a place that I have only ever dreamed of touching and experiencing.

Frankly, if I could get here, anyone can get here.

I have decided to share my tools and my epiphanies and my insights and my narrative in the hope that it might help other souls—other MEs—come home to themselves: to the unique expressions of the Universe they were designed to be.

When I began my spiritual journey in earnest at nineteen, I read a few books and went to a few seminars, and then I did some mushrooms and dipped a toe into the vastness of creation. I thought, *DANG, I'm the shit. This stuff is amazing. Anything is possible and I am awake and alive.* Shortly after that initial awakening, however, I entered what I now call the righteous, spiritualist phase. *OUCH!*

Man, this phase is painful. It's the one where we become *better than, more than,* and think we are enlightened to truths that others should just know, *dammit.* "Stop doing this or that," we command. "Can't you see what you're doing? You're messing with my vibe. You're polluting my chakras (or whatever). You're killing my buzz, man."

I stayed in the righteous spiritualist phase for a while. Far longer than I care to admit. I stayed in it until I realized that I was just another judgmental asshole, and in being so, was no different than any other judgmental asshole who feels justified in his judgment because of his religious or political or cultural beliefs. I learned that judgment is judgment, hate is hate, and struggle is struggle no matter what belief or myth you are defending at the time or how justified or right you think you are.

Once I emerged from spiritual righteousness (and eventually stopped punishing myself for it), I took a bit of a break and tried just to fit in again. I tried to take what I had learned and live among the Muggles, just a little happier, a little more authentically ME than before.

I still had not fully returned home to myself or achieved escape velocity from the mundane and mediocre. For years yet, I would fall and fail and struggle and rage and laugh and cry and hurt and get hurt. I'd sleep-create and awaken. I'd get drunk AGAIN. Take up smoking "socially, of course" AGAIN. I'd let my impeccable diet go, AGAIN. My pendulum would swing from one extreme to another, but in ever-slighter, decreasing degrees with each pass. That was progress.

Whenever I got righteous and bossy and dared to step on my soapbox, the Universe in all her loving kindness and benevolence would knock me on my ass, landing me right back in my own stinky mess. Whereupon she'd just point at me and laugh.

I'd get angry and shake my fists and ask, "Why me?" and "Why this?" And sometimes I'd wonder if I would have the strength to get up again. Literally. Sometimes I just gave in to my brokenness and said, "Maybe I'm not fixable." At that perfect moment, the Universe would send hope to get me up and going again.

My point is this . . . I'm human and so I am by design perfectly imperfect. I am extraordinary and I am utterly ordinary. I am significant and I am utterly insignificant. I am broken and I am whole. And I am here, now, living my life on this planet we call Earth, and this living thing is messy. I mean the shit is seriously messy.

When it's beautiful, DAMN it's beautiful.

When it's messy, it is full-body gag, disgustingly smelly and vile.

I have yet to meet a perfect human. A whole human. I don't think they exist. I see a lot of people trying to convince me they are perfect, but then . . . wait for it . . . their broken bits emerge. They always do.

And I have yet to see a perfect relationship, yet many of us are still searching for it—for that one "perfect" love until death do us part. Why?

What if we are perfect, just as we are? What if every relationship is perfect? What if there is no one true love, but many?

Here is what I can promise as we embark on the journey of *Potentialized*. I will continue to be human with all that it entails. I will continue to live until I don't. What will be will be and I will do better and be better when I can, but when I don't or I'm not I will forgive myself, and then I will get up and do it again.

And when I remember who I am, when I am the ME the universe created me to be, I will look around at you, my fellow humans, and offer you my hand or my shoulder, and I will seek yours to pull me through to the other side. I promise to share the gifts and the sparks that the Universe so graciously sprinkled among us with you, and I will give you the opportunity to share yours and to shine. And together we will rise.

Together we will remember who we are.

Together we will sing our unique singularities into the symphony of creation, because we cannot *not* do so.

The music we create together brings tears to the eyes of our Creator because she loves us so completely and deeply and unwaveringly, always and in all ways.

I have fallen in love with humanity. This is a love I never knew or thought I would know in this lifetime. Because of this love, I pledge my service to you and to our awakening—and I know that we can and will awaken.

We are! Right Now! Awakening! All of us.

We are potentialized.

We are potentializing.

And we are potentializers, helping each other to rise!

CHAPTER THREE

WHO ARE WE REALLY?

I am the ocean awakened within the drop of water.

We are singular, unique expressions of a multifaceted, intelligent, loving universe experiencing creation through us. We are creators at the leading edge of creation, simultaneously creating and experiencing our creations. We are integral threads in the fabric of All That Is. We are immensely significant, yet within the entire realm of the infinite Universe, we are entirely insignificant. It is in the tension of reconciling these two realities that we struggle to find our place, meaning, and opportunities for contribution to the whole—our significance. Keeping our egos in check, our utter insignificance is there to remind us not to take ourselves too seriously and instill in us a sense of divine humility.

All things are connected and equally divine. No thing, big or small, holds more significance than any other. No human beings, no matter their positions, religious beliefs, colors, nationalities, professions, or wealth, are more or less than any other. We are all born, we all die, as the world turns and the Universe breathes in and out and continues her exploration and discovery of herself. Each of us at death returns to the field of All That Is like a drop of water returning to the ocean, and then, once again, we are born and reemerge into the illusion of singularity, as a drop, in a different time and place.

I rediscovered this knowing when I was gazing into the infinite night sky, knowing that there are TRILLIONS of galaxies. That's when I realized that all that we struggle with here on this tiny speck called Earth—all the things we fight for, rage against, love, hate, accept, judge—none of it matters to anything or anyone but us.

When we look at the Earth from outer space, first as a beautiful green and blue globe, and then from far enough away to reduce it to a speck in the vast darkness of the void of space, we don't see war, we don't see pollution, we don't see kind acts or cruel acts, we don't see politics or economics or cultures or money. We just see beauty and silence. We observe existence without human drama.

The starlit night sky gave me perspective and begged the questions: "Why does this or anything matter? What am I fighting for? Why do I need to be 'right' or 'better' or 'good' or 'bad'? What does it all mean? Who am I and who are we in the grand scheme? What role do we play in the Universe's grand plan?" And when I asked these questions I got an answer. The simplicity of it shook my reality to the core. The Universe spoke and said, "You are a singular expression of the Creator sent forth into the realm of all creation to experience what WE have collectively created. Every emotion, every permutation of behavior, and every experience possible, all of it is feeding the Creator's knowing of OUR SELVES.

"You cannot err. Being is all that is asked of you. Create whatever you want. You cannot get it wrong. To know love, the Creator must know hate. To know ease, the Creator must know struggle. To know beauty, the Creator must experience ugliness."

It took me a while to fully comprehend the enormity of this transmission. Years actually. At first, I couldn't take it in fully. It made me angry and excited. I was saddened and overwhelmed by too much freedom. The Universe had given me enough rope to hang myself a gazillion times. I argued against the message I'd heard and feared the truth of it. It felt to me like humanity had been given free will and we'd messed up. We'd used our incredible powers of creation only to create chaos and suffering and disease.

I looked around at my own life and I saw the quality of my creation and I was not pleased. Yet I realized that all of it was exactly as I'd created it to be, exactly as WE had created it to be.

And I asked myself, *How did I get here? How did I create this?*

The answer came (as it always does when we truly allow ourselves to listen), and, as always, it was simple: I created my reality one thought, one word, and one action at a time. My reality was the sum total of all the thoughts, words, and actions I had thought/said/taken from the time I was born to the present.

But wait, I insisted. *I couldn't have chosen this!* Then I traced my life back and I saw the choices I had made. I saw the thoughts that lead to the emotions that lead to the words that lead to the actions which, when strung together, had created my life exactly as it was in that perfect moment.

And then I went bigger. I realized that reality—by which I mean the collective reality that humanity is experiencing—is the result of our collective thoughts, emotions, words, and actions. This recognition brought me to my knees. I was humbled by the power we hold individually and collectively, saddened by what we'd done with it and yet hopeful because I saw that I/WE could do something about it starting right now.

I cannot change what is behind me. It has already happened. I must let it go, surrender to it, forgive myself, forgive others, and LOVE IT for its perfection because it could not be any other way than what it is *or it would be.*

I was brought to this awakening, this knowing that now I can choose consciously. I can stop the creative process and choose my next thought. I can choose the quality of it and the content of it.

Who am I and who is this seer of thought? I wondered. I thought I was my thoughts. In identifying with them, I merge with them. But I also can stop them, interrupt them, witness them, change them, CHOOSE THEM! I have seen that I am the knower behind my thoughts. I am the ocean awakened within the drop of water! I am free. And yet nothing has changed except my perspective of who and what I am and what I am capable of.

I am the UNIVERSE. I can create heaven with my very next thought if I choose. I can see beauty in all that is beautiful AND all that is ugly and I can allow both to exist side by side and witness their perfection. I am free to be without judgment or I can judge—but knowing this, why would I choose the restriction and separation of judgment? I wouldn't. That is, unless I forget and get lost again in the singularity of separation. And I do get lost again, and again and again (and I know that I will get lost many more times before I take my last breath), I will forgive myself each time. I will forgive myself as I remember and awaken, which is ever more frequently than it used to be.

Each moment that arises is new and fresh and full of possibility. Each moment is a blank canvas on which to paint any reality we choose. It is our choice and it has always been our choice. We have simply forgotten this whenever we felt swept away with the emotions and beliefs that seemingly chose our reality for us.

Struggling is prevalent, but always optional. You can stop struggling any time you want and you can wake up to what you are creating and choose to create whatever you want. Power beyond measure, endless possibilities, dreams fulfilled, or nightmares realized—it does not matter! All experience expands OUR knowledge of OUR creation.

True inspiration always comes to us from the Divine, after which we filter it through mind, perception, judgment, fear, and mental programming until it is unrecognizable. But we can learn to recognize divine inspiration when it comes. And if we can allow it to expand and be without the obstruction of fear or too much thought, then miracles will be the result.

Our purpose cannot be discovered through the mind, as it is the mind that takes us from that path. Our purpose will be (re)discovered in dreaming, silence, and doing the little things we do that bring us joy.

There was always a point in our lives—usually early—where our purpose was expressing itself. We knew. And then we either talked ourselves out of it over time, because it did not seem practical, or let someone close to us talk us out of it either by directly telling us it was impossible or through comments of disapproval. Rubbish! There is no such thing as impractical or impossible. If we can think it, it can be done—somehow, someway.

Reach back in time, before you were discouraged, and ask your knowing self what it wants to do in the world. Then be patient and listen for the answer: It will come and you will remember. And when you do remember, you will probably experience emotions like fear and sadness at having given up on this path. You may also experience tears of joy at the remembering. Once you've touched it again—that desired experience—a new journey can begin: a journey aligned with your deepest desire, your heart, and your soul's purpose.

This convergence of heart's desire and soul's purpose is one of the most powerful places you will ever touch inside yourself. Anchor yourself there, daily, until the vision of it becomes as real as anything else in your life. Until it becomes your true north. Then reset your life compass and move toward it one step at a time.

Don't be discouraged by how far the journey seems. The journey to realize our soul's purpose is not linear. There are many shortcuts and miraculous leaps that we only discover once we are brave enough to walk the path.

What is most important is just to walk. To put one foot in front of the other on the path toward this place that makes your heart sing. The whole of the Universe will conspire on your behalf to help get you there, and ease and grace will return to your life, the color will return to your cheeks, and music will return to the silence. And the journey to realizing this potential will be as rich and warm and exciting as the eventual getting there is, because you will experience the magic of creation along the way and it will restore your faith in what is possible, in people, in yourself.

The YOU that navigates the world each day on this path of remembering and rediscovery will be one that sparkles and shines with a smile of deep knowing that there truly is magic in the world. This YOU knows that the only thing we need to do to activate it is to align with our purpose and move toward it.

The Universe's deepest desire for each of us is that we sing our uniquely beautiful and singular note into the symphony of All That Is and to shine our brilliant light as brightly as we possibly can. That is the greatest gift we can give HER and ourselves and all of humanity and the Earth. So discover, sing, dance, and shine, and help others to do the same and we will see the world transformed. We will see and experience heaven on earth NOW regardless of what is happening in the broader world of politics, economics, and religion.

Our world and our Universe shine with the light of the Divine in full expression of herself becoming and expanding through us.

CHAPTER FOUR

FRIENDS DON'T LET FRIENDS SLEEP AND CREATE

*Every new day is buzzing and popping
with pure potentiality.*

Sleep-creating is the act of creating while under the influence of forgetfulness. When we forget that we are God and that we are the unique and powerful creators of every moment of our reality then it is our fears, patterns, programs, stories, myths, and beliefs that create for us. They drive the creation bus—and a creation bus driven under the influence of forgetfulness (DUIF) should be pulled over immediately and cited for recklessly creating a reality that we pray daily will change to reflect what we "really want."

When we sleep create, we CTRL C + CTRL V the reality from the moment before into another moment, then another, then another and another, and so on. It sounds tedious, doesn't it? That's because it is. As well as ridiculous, considering how much time, energy, and money we spend trying to change our realities with books and seminars and therapy and complaining and lamenting and struggling and hoping and praying to try and make things different than they are.

And what do we do? We fall asleep to who we are, get in the driver's seat of our creation bus anyhow, and drive it off the cliff . . . AGAIN.

You can actually see this happening all around us in our culture, in the media and in our daily lives. Oh, the drudgery of it. Lather, rinse, repeat. Another day, another dollar. Alarm, UGH, routine, work, home, routine, bed, reset alarm, UGH . . .

Silly humans, praying and pleading for a better life, a different life, and all the while CTRL C + CTRL Ving through every moment of a new day and whizzing that creation bus right past the choice points and opportunities that would allow us, the creators, to make a different choice and alter course. Every new day is teaming with new possibilities—literally an infinite number of choices that would lead to different outcomes, new and more delightful realities.

Every new day is buzzing and popping with pure potentiality. And what do we do? We sleep-create our way through it while praying for change.

Well, clearly that doesn't work.

So wake up. SLAP! SLAP! SLAP!

No, I'm not going to be gentle about it. Has gentle worked? Have the books worked? Have the seminars and the therapy sessions and all the praying in the world worked? NO. Because you're here reading this, I know you're still searching. And if you say, "Wait, but *this* book taught me *this* or I learned *that* in *that* seminar, or I had a breakthrough in therapy," I will say, "Yes, YOU did. And any benefit or change or relief was the result of you answering the call of a teacher (through their book, seminar, or retreat), integrating the gift, and then choosing to think or speak or act differently as a result, which means YOU created a new reality because you integrated new information or new learnings that made you think, speak, and act differently than before."

It's not the other way around. The book didn't do it. The seminar didn't do it. YOU did it.

HOORAY FOR YOU!

I'm serious. I'm jumping up and down with pompoms and cheering you on because YOU woke up and created from a conscious place, a different place than before, and so you changed the trajectory of your life. You changed what's possible. You are potentializing on the path to a new destination!

You have the opportunity and capacity to do this in every moment—in the smallest and the biggest ways. You could turn to a person beside you right now and simply smile and say hello. Start a conversation. Or you could hold the door open for someone behind you. Or you could stop, take a breath, look around, and find something beautiful in that moment: a reason to be grateful, a reason to laugh, a reason to cry. Or you could just be still and observe humanity or nature in action. These are small things, but they can create big changes over time if they become part of your regular behavior, because they are spontaneous. The Universe lives in spontaneity. Opportunity is found through spontaneity. All of nature is spontaneous. Join the dance and discover new possibilities and opportunities. Spontaneity breaks the drudgery and monotony and destroys the probability of a CTRL C + CTRL V day of sleep-creating.

You can also go bigger—or even just think about going bigger—by understanding how much power for change and transformation you have in every moment. If you're in a job you hate or a relationship that is sucking the life out of you or you have friends that can only see the person you've been and won't allow room for the person you are becoming, you can change any of these experiences in an instant through the simple act of choosing.

People do this all the time. Usually when things become so painful that they just can't take it anymore that gives them the impetus to up and quit or break up or tell off a friend. But we don't have to wait until this painful point. We already have a choice in any moment to either change what is, change ourselves, or jump ship entirely, swim to the nearest shore, and start over again. Any of these options is perfectly acceptable.

The point here is that in order to choose to create a new possibility or outcome you have to wake yourself up from your habitual sleep-creating, take a look around you, and make a conscious choice. This is the only way out of the CTRL C + CTRL V loop.

When there is a fire, you stop, drop, and roll.

When you catch yourself sleep-creating you have to stop, awaken, and choose.

It's that simple.

If you're frustrated by all this power and ability you apparently have, but can't seem to access when you want it, then we can assume you are one of the billions of people sleep-creating who want to stop doing so.

Good. You're in the right place. Reading these words now will help you wake your ass up so you don't drive your creation bus into a pole and then have to exclaim, yet again, "Shit! Look at this mess."

Trust me, I've crashed my bus so many times it's a wonder I'm still here and not lying in a hospital bed somewhere in a coma resulting from terminal brain damage. You would think I'd have gotten the message that sleep-creating is dangerous after the one-millionth time I crashed my creation bus and after the thousands of humans I plowed into, but NOOOOOOO.

Apparently I'm not only a silly human, I'm also stubborn.

That's why we have to work together to help wake each other up from this tedious and potential consuming process. Friends don't let friends sleep-create.

CHAPTER FIVE

CHOOSE YOU

*At the center of all you desire
all that you pray for and want is YOU.*

Every moment is an opportunity to choose and therefore to create your life. You can also flip this around to say that every moment creates your life. Your life is the sum total of all the moments you've lived and all the choices you've made.

You stand at the leading edge of your creation. The cursor is blinking. The canvas is fresh and white. And the Universe is asking, "Where to now? What shall WE create next?" She will happily and lovingly and willingly be a conspirator in YOUR creation and a copilot on your creation bus.

How benevolent OUR Universe is.. No matter what has come before, who you've been, what you've done, SHE lovingly and without judgment asks, "Where are we going today and how can I help?" This depth of unconditional love literally brings me to tears. The Creator loves the piece of herself in YOU that was sent forth into this specific reality at this specific time to experience her creation—OUR creation. We are given full permission to play, laugh, cry, feel, scream, dance, lift up, tear down, create, and destroy . . . without judgment . . . only with love. Always.

One of my favorite phrases was shared by my friend Peter. He said, "You are so becoming." Nothing could be truer and more powerful than this simple statement. We ARE all so becoming in every moment. We are potentialized and potentializing. But even so, most of us sleep-create our way through our own becoming.

Well, wake up! The world and humanity (and dare I say the Universe) need you to be the best YOU you can be. Creation is a symphony of souls, all contributing their singular notes of unique expression. If we all contribute the note of sameness (and shoulds and conformity), then the symphony of creation suffers from mediocrity and dullness, and to the ear of the Universe it probably sounds a bit like a monkey banging on a keyboard. All because humans are choosing to express something other than the extraordinary, divine, authentic, unique, radiant brilliance they were created to be.

To this I say, "Silly, silly humans." Thank ME (and YOU/US) that this moment is a fresh new moment in which to choose the quality of the note you contribute to the symphony of life. Be you, find you, sing or play you loudly and proudly, and then the Conductor of All That Is will smile, nod, and rejoice while conducting the most infinitely beautiful, infinitely complex, infinitely mind/heart/life-blowing piece of music creation has ever known.

And that, fellow humans, is why the Universe selfishly and tirelessly and with gigglingly silly glee conspires with you and for you to become YOU and CHOOSE YOU (and only YOU) in every moment of every day that you are alive on this fabulous planet.

So I say please, as the Universe expressing herself through Bradley Robert Thomason (which basically means YOU expressing a piece of yourself through Bradley Thomason to remind yourself of this in this very moment), sing your note and play your instrument so that I can hear you and see you and encourage you and love you and appreciate you in every moment as you become more YOU. As you consciously choose the path that leads you back home to all that you've ever wanted, all you've been searching for, all that your heart desires, and all that your soul has longed for in all the books and seminars and therapy sessions and psychedelic experiences, come back home to YOU. YOU are the authentic, brilliant, radiant, singular self you've been seeking. Come home to yourself—to the self that the Universe created in all its authenticity and pure beauty.

I dare you to do YOU with everything you've got.

And I want to remind you that who YOU are is not what you do or what you have or who you are friends with or how many resources you have access to.

Stop searching and start being YOU right now, wherever

YOU are, whatever YOU are, however YOU are; and if you choose to do so, then choose to do YOU better in this moment. This is potentializing.

At the center of all you desire, all that you pray for and want is YOU. But here is the catch: If you are not living authentically as YOU would like to live, nothing you desire will bring you satisfaction or fulfillment. No relationship, no job, no amount of money, no material possession, no event, and no circumstance. YOU require nothing to be potentialized other than the full expression of YOU.

THAT IS ALL.

You might want to pause here and read the above a few times. Let it sink in. Put the book down, take a walk, and then come back and read it again. This is the core truth of this book. You are the one you've been waiting for. YOU ARE THE ANSWER to your prayers and desires and wants.

We are taught that we must seek or do or achieve or be what others want us to be in order to be happy and fulfilled, but this is a LIE. The ONLY thing that will fulfill you is coming home to the YOU the Universe created you to be. PERIOD. Anything else will only give you temporary relief from the misery of you not living or being or expressing YOU. You cannot potentialize the inauthentic you, the "should" you, the you that you think others want you to be.

Certainly you can try to potentialize this you—lord knows, I tried and tried and tried, and the result was only more misery and suffering–but your efforts will fail. No relief or joy will come. If you say, "But I am being the ME the Universe created me to be" and you are still wishing for a new job or a new love or more money or better health, then I can assure you that you are potentializing a false version of you that is not the YOU the Universe created you to be. When you come home to YOU, it is an experience of joy and beauty and sweetness and knowing that just bursts forth or bubbles up from the depths of your being. You FEEL it, you REMEMBER it. Your being aligns with its source and your soul aligns with the Universe and there is no resistance, no suffering, no wanting or needing, only the desire to express

YOU better in each moment and serve the Universe in any way She desires.

You don't have to change careers or relationships or outfits to be you. Just be YOU and play with the discovery of yourself such that you discover yourself more and better each moment and each day. And when you don't like the you that shows up in a moment or a day . . . forgive yourself and do better in the next moment or the next day. Because you can and you will. You need only choose it and your life will blossom and opportunities will come and people will be drawn to your YOU-ness. 'Cause there is no other YOU in all the Universe and all She desires is you to be the best and purist and most radiant YOU that ever is, was, or will be.

WAKE UP and do YOU with power, conviction, and grace always and in all ways.

Somewhere inside, you know and remember the authentic YOU I'm talking about. You know this self! You know YOU! For me, it was little Brad at seven years old before the pain of life made itself known. Such a loving, open, special, divine being he was—like an angel among humans. I spent practically my whole life searching for him only to find out that he had always been with me. He never left me. I left him. Life happened.

When life experiences hurt me, my mind tried to create meaning out of them, but it couldn't because my mind was trying to understand things that it could not possibly understand as it had only developed for seven years. It did not have the capacity to understand the darker side of humanity yet. But now it does and so that program that was written by the mind to make sense of a painful experience LONG gone by no longer serves me. When I realize this and free myself from it I am freer to choose and be ME in every moment because the old program is no longer choosing for me.

My mind now understands the human condition better. It's clear to me that every human is potentialized in every moment, which means people are doing their best or else they would do things differently. I know that all people write programs, similar to the one Little Brad wrote, to make sense of their realities.

And just as my program ran my life and separated me from ME, their programs are running their lives and separating them from THEM—and usually they just don't know it. I know I didn't. Until I did.

We are all products of our histories, our pains and pleasures, our experiences, including abuse and loss. But we are NOT our history, our pains, our pleasures, our experiences, or our abuses. We are not our stories or our myths. We are the singular radiant notes that the Universe sent forth into this reality to sing and to experience OUR creation.

It is time to KNOW this and choose to come home to ourselves. RIGHT NOW. No excuses. Don't waste another moment allowing the programs or stories you created to make sense of reality create more mediocrity, pain, and suffering for US.

In the next moment, and the next, and the next, let us introduce into the field of pure potentiality a thought and a word and an action that reflects this truth. In this way, the caterpillar that is humanity will be transformed into a butterfly.

CHAPTER SIX

BETWEEN YOU AND YOU

Just because you are feeling FEAR
does not mean that what you are afraid of is real.

I f each of us has an innate force seeking to express itself fully through US as US, then why do we struggle so? Why does it seem that the longest journey we take in this life is the journey home to ourselves? Mine was a thirty-year journey from when I consciously set out. I am counting from the first step I took on the path.

As I took that first step, I had no idea of where I was going or where it would lead me.

Looking back at the end of the thirty-year journey, after discovering that I was what I was searching for all along, I asked the questions: What kept me from me? What dimmed my radiance? What muted my note? What inhibited me from expressing the seed of the Universe that lives within me?

With her typical joy, generosity, kindness, and love, the Universe answered me, saying, "Dear one, there is really only one thing standing in the way of you being the YOU I created you to be, and that is fear: fear of rejection, fear of being different, fear of being ridiculed, fear of death, fear of abandonment, fear of suffering, fear of going without, fear of being unlovable, fear of _____ (fill in the blank). Fear keeps you from being and expressing the truth of who and what you are and why you are here."

Her answer hit home as I looked around and realized that I was trapped inside a prison of fear and judgment. And what is judgment if not an expression of fear? The simplicity of this was too much for my mind to wade through and comprehend, so it immediately started to defend itself saying it was just trying to protect me, keep me safe, and prevent me from being hurt or judged or left alone. Seen from a different perspective, it was just trying to make sure I would be accepted and loved and successful and included.

All this is true. It had tried to do all this. "But," I asked, "dear mind, have you succeeded? Have I not felt pain and failure and separation and hurt anyway? Has protecting me worked? Have we avoided what you sought to avoid?" To which there was no answer to consider except no.

"That's OK," I said. "Thank you for trying, you've done only what you thought was best for US and I love you for it. Deeply. But it may now be time to try something different—to be afraid AND to move forward instead of recoil or move away from whatever it is we think we are afraid of. What if we formed a different relationship with fear? What if we challenged fear and questioned fear and sought to understand the forms it takes to trick us and imprison us and keep us from US? Maybe it is time to challenge our limitations and emancipate us from them."

Please make note that it is not by mistake that I speak to my mind like it is separate from me. Each of us is running a similar mental dialogue every day, even if we are not aware of it. If we disrupt the autopilot thinking of the mind by questioning it, we quickly realize that we can reason with it and free ourselves from the restrictions it imposes on us. But who is dialoguing with whom? For me personally, it feels as though my true, essential self is, my knower or Creator, dialoguing with the human mind self; and depending on whom I align myself with, I will either remain imprisoned or I will notice that the key to my own emancipation is in my grasp and I will set myself free.

As I started to look more closely at fear and see how powerful and insidious it was in my thinking and creating, I sought to understand the roots of the fear. Where was fear born, where did it come from? Was my fear different from his or hers or yours? What forms did fear take? And I began to draw some conclusions.

FEAR

While many books have been published about fear, its forms, and how to move beyond it, I would like to share with you my personal perspective as a human being who is waking up to my potential and understanding better how to jailbreak my radiance from the prison of fear in order to set it free to be and express and sing and fly and dance.

I have found that almost all forms and roots of fear are constructs of the mind, and 99.9 percent of the things I fear happening are not objectively real or true dangers. One way to test this is to look at ALL the many fearful thoughts we think, and then look around at all the things others fear. If you can think about it—a scenario or an object, such as a plant or insect or animal or weather pattern—some human somewhere is deathly afraid of it. Fears can become pathologies that make some people's lives so small that they literally cannot leave their houses. And there are some people who seem to have no fears at all. They are bold and adventurous and take one risk after another. Such is the spectrum of fear in human experience.

What is real? If there are so many varieties and types and degrees and intensities of fear, what is objectively true about fear? I believe fear is a construct of the mind. Fears arise in the mind, and then, like any other thoughts, we choose to override them or to believe them. The human body experiences a biological and chemical response to whichever choice we make. The simple fact that there is no absolute truth or consistency about things people fear means that most of the things we fear are not true threats, and that our minds have made up reasons to fear these so-called threats or adopted or constructed our fears of them or learned to be afraid of them just for ourselves.

Let's dig a little deeper into fear.

The only true and acceptable fear is an instinctual fear, one that arises based on an external stimulus that indicates possible or imminent danger to our survival, such as the smell of smoke, which might signify that the house is on fire. Look at the natural world and you will find many examples of instinctual fears that help protect us from injury or death. These are part of the brain's "wiring" and biologically designed for our self-preservation. Such fears elicit an IMMEDIATE fight-or-flight response in the body. When this response is triggered, a series of hormones is released that initiate physiological changes to help us get to safety or end danger as quickly as possible.

In fight-or-flight situations, the mind doesn't have time to consciously think or process information—there is only stimulus and response! The physiological changes can be so extreme that people have been known to find the strength to lift cars off of their loved ones when this kind of fear hits. Imagine if they had stopped to think, *That's a car! I can't lift that car, that's impossible.* It would have been if they weren't reacting to danger spontaneously with a rush of hormones in their bloodstreams.

When danger is extreme, the mind doesn't have time to engage. We respond by pure instinct. And what happens when pure instinct is neither diminished nor debated by thought? Superhuman things are often accomplished, that's what.

Unfortunately, the mind has perverted our basic innate fears to manipulate us. It creates all kinds of fictitious scenarios to elicit the fight-or-flight response and make us back away from a situation or a person it perceives as an imminent threat. But when we take a closer look at these fears and analyze them, we usually will find that the mind has made up a "what if" scenario and scared the crap out of us with it to prevent us from making a decision or engaging in some behavior it sees as POTENTIALLY dangerous. Here's the gotcha: These perverted fears are based on what the mind THINKS is dangerous or threatening and not what actually IS dangerous or threatening.

There is a big difference between real danger and imagined danger. What the mind thinks is dangerous could be based on an old program that was installed by some previous experience. For instance, if you were attacked by a dog when you were a youngster, your mind might perceive ALL dogs of similar size or look to be dangerous and therefore it makes you afraid of them ALL rather than what is actually true which is that some dogs are dangerous and many are not.

Each situation must be assessed as it arises to determine risk.

Fears of "what ifs" or worst-case scenarios are by far the biggest impediments to leading a fully potentialized life. Because YOU fears nothing or no one and would never do anything to endanger or harm you, you can trust that if you are tapped in, tuned in, and turned on to the universal frequency within you then you will know what to say, where to go, how to prepare, and what to do in each moment, effortlessly and with precision and clarity.

Without our unrealistic fears, our lives would be easy and joyful and fulfilled. So why, in our current potentialized states, do we feel like failures, or inadequate or not successful enough in some area of our lives, be it our relationships, finances, professions, physical health, or whatever? It is because we are afraid we might fail, or be alone, or be judged, or be broken, or look bad, or look like we don't know, or, or, or . . . again, fill in the blank. Although the truth is that none of these fears is realistic we buy in to them because the mind is so persuasive and because we FEEL fear as real. If we FEEL it, we believe it must be so.

Yes, I can feel fear in my body. Yes, you can, too. You can also feel afraid when watching a scary movie, which is a biological response to light shining through celluloid or a digital broadcast with a sound track. Do you see? Feeling "fear" does not make something real.

Let me say that again, just because you are feeling FEAR does not mean that what you are afraid of is real or that the feeling of fear itself is real. It is just an emotional, biological, chemical response to a thought or experience. THAT IS ALL.

All around me every day I see people imposing unrealistic and fictitious fears on themselves and others. I understand these fears, I really do. Usually they arise with the best of intentions, to keep us or others safe from perceived danger. But just because we are afraid of some "what if" or worst-case scenario does not make the fear real. The trouble is that our fears for ourselves and others limit our expression, limit our experiences, inhibit our exploration, and rob us of our ability to choose the thoughts, words, and actions that create our reality.

Unfortunately, most people these days do not have a conscious relationship with their fears and so they allow fear to run their lives. When they feel afraid of whatever they fear, they inhibit the behavior of themselves and others in order to alleviate the fears created by their own minds. This is a crime against self and a crime against others who are simply trying to come home to themselves whether or not they know it.

We must develop a new relationship with fear. We must challenge it. Question it. We must talk to the mind and ask if a given fear is real. We must examine it and see how it persuades us, traps us, and keeps us where we are or imprisoned in mediocrity, and prevents us from actualizing our potential in the next moment. And because real fear, the fear designed to carry us away from real danger, happens so quickly and without the ability for the mind to get in the way, I can with a great degree of certainty say that MOST of our fears are not real. In fact, I would say 99.9 percent of them are manufactured by the mind.

Let that sink in.

To the mind, the unknown is much scarier than the known, even if what is known is barely tolerable to us anymore. What is possible, truly possible, ALWAYS lies outside our comfort zone. ALWAYS. When the pain of staying where we are becomes greater than the fear of leaving where we are for realities unknown we will override fear and act boldly—finally. But why wait for that much pain before taking action? Why not examine the fear, see that it is not real, AND determine that it serves only to make the mind feel safe because it is protecting us from harm like a parent protecting its child.

It is time for our adult selves to say to the mind, "I have got this. I know you are afraid, but your fear is keeping us small and stuck and I desire to be more, do more, and feel more. And if I fail, so what? I will not use that as an excuse not to try again. I will choose boldly because that is the adventure called life." Choosing boldly makes our lives interesting. Choosing boldly makes the impossible possible and ensures that our potential is rising and blossoming and exploding into new possibilities.

FEAR EXERCISE

I want you to take a moment to dream. I want you to dream big, bold dreams for yourself. I find that if you are not scared, you are not dreaming big enough. Dream of and feel the life you want. Ask the Universe who knows YOU better than anyone to show you your BIGGEST purpose and potential. While you are in the dreaming, be careful not to let the mind jump in and start arguing the reasons why you cannot have whatever it is you are dreaming of having. That will come later in the exercise. For now, just dream, and if you like, write it down. Once you have it, once you've touched it, put it down.

Then start thinking of what you need to do to go from where you are now to there—to the place in time when your dream has been realized. Let the mind say whatever it wants and be hyperaware of what it is saying. Write the thoughts down or speak them out loud and record them. Don't try and dialogue with the mind, just let it riff until it is done. Then know this, every one of the fears that the mind threw at you, every one of the limitations or impediments it created, was false. You haven't even taken step one toward your dream yet, so no one, not YOU, your mind, or anyone else, knows what you will encounter on the journey to your dream realized. Any guess or supposition is fictitious and while it may seem real or inevitable, it is not, because it has not even happened yet.

Now look back and think of all the times your mind scared you into inaction and held you back. You probably can even conjure memories where your mind made you cripplingly afraid of a what-if reality and you proceeded anyway and the what-if never happened. Maybe you got a great job or met an amazing friend or lover despite your mind working to keep you afraid from moving toward it.

When you complete the exercise, forgive your mind and thank it. It really is only trying to protect you, but you are able to protect yourself. If you want to live into your Divine potential, you need to learn to leap into the void when the Universe says leap (whether or not you are afraid) and experience that she always has you and will never let you fail or fall.

Fear is not the only obstacle that stands between you and YOU. Besides fear, other constructs impede the full realization of our potential. We are a species born with less instinct than any other. We are born helpless, unable to feed or care for ourselves and with little innate knowing about how to be human. Thus the miraculous and infinitely wondrous mind learns and observes, learns and observes, and in doing so, slowly, but increasingly guides our behavior in subtle and unconscious ways that over time can SERIOUSLY inhibit our becoming. This is how the mind keeps us trapped in mediocrity and sameness and using only a fraction of our divine potential.

I have identified three constructs that I find have been impediments to me living and expressing my potential. These concepts are not new; they've been around for a while. As a human learning better how to live, but not a human trained in the field of psychology, I'm going to share them as I came to know them in the hope that they may also help you to emancipate yourself from the power they wield in inhibiting your becoming.

PATTERNS

Patterns by definition are recurrent ways of behaving toward a given object or situation. Patterns form through repetition. We are not born with them. We either learn them from our family or our friends, society, or another cultural group, or we just develop them through repetition. The longer a pattern is repeated, the more rigid it becomes. The more patterns we have guiding us through the day, the less free we are to meet each moment with spontaneity when it asks us to dance with it.

Some people are so stuck in their patterned behaviors that they leave no space for anyone or anything new to come in, and yet daily they pray for someone or something new. See their dilemma? Patterns, like fears, make our worlds small and provide very little in the way of opportunities for anything different to enter.

The Universe is in flow; we see flow everywhere. She is a powerful force, but she is not going to work extra hard, against you just for you, to bring you what you say you want when you leave no room for it to come in and are not willing to step into a new moment with freedom and spontaneity to claim it. Therefore, the Universe celebrates your rigidity and remains, in every moment, eager and ready to bring new possibilities if and when you provide the opening and flexibility to allow them.

Beware your patterns. ANY patterns. Like fear, they feel like our friends. They make life easier and safer, but one by one they trap us into living in ever-smaller realities. Gradually we become less bold, less adventurous, less adaptable, less fluid, and less able to meet the spontaneity of each moment. Then, if we find ourselves wishing for new or different experiences, we have to become willing to let go of our pattern "friends" to make room for what we are longing and praying for.

PATTERN EXERCISE

Identify your patterns big and small. Write them down. Keep a running list.

Once you start looking for them, you will most likely find more than you imagined you had. How do you start each day? Do you always make the coffee first? Shower? Take the dog out? Go for a run? Where do you eat lunch?

Do you eat lunch? What do you do when you get home from work? These are patterns. What would happen if you broke them and do something else different tomorrow? Would you feel uncomfortable?

The stronger a pattern, the more uncomfortable you will feel when you try and break it.

Strong patterns almost take on a force and life of their own. They demand that we do them on schedule and in the right order or they will make us very uncomfortable. Some people can actually feel dizzy if they break a pattern; that is how strong patterns are. Breaking a pattern can often feel as awkward as writing with your non-dominant hand.

Do you always take the same route to work? To the gym? What would happen if you didn't? Imagine how many new places and people you would experience.

Do you go to the same place for coffee every day? What would happen if you tried someplace new?

New relationships, experiences, and possibilities emerge when we choose to do something different in this moment than we habitually do. And better yet, when we allow the universal knowing inside us to guide our thinking, speaking, and doing such that in each moment we remain open to where the flow wants to take us.

Challenge your patterns, even the small ones. Liberate yourself from their inflexibility. You can find flow in each moment and in each day by allowing yourself to be guided fluidly by YOU rather than rigidly by you. If you let some of your patterns drop away, potentializing will become a powerful and exciting adventure full of miracles.

So now that you've identified some of your patterns, break them. Do the opposite. Challenge them. Ask the Universe or the knowing in you what to do in the next moment. Be spontaneous and let the Universe know you are doing this so that she can help you create something different and more aligned with YOU in the next moment. Do this for a day, a week, a month, but be careful you do not create new patterns. The more you free yourself, the more you invite the flow into your life to inform and guide your behaviors and choices and the more you will hop and skip from impulse to impulse and synchronicity to synchronicity.

PROGRAMS

After we are born, we remain dependent on our parents (or their surrogates) for longer than the offspring of any other species on the planet. Some baby birds are born helpless, but within six weeks they mature enough to take care of themselves and create families of their own. Some animals, like horses, have to be able to literally run for their lives within hours of being born. But humans take a long time to grow to sufficient maturity that we are able to take care of our own basic needs. While I'm no scientist, I would argue that this is because we are the most complex organism on the planet physically and neurologically. I believe it is the latter aspect of who we are that requires us to remain dependent as long as we do. Our brains need the time to learn and adapt to functioning and living in this place.

Both our "hardware" (the body) and "software" (the mind) are immature at birth, but still capable of producing the trillions of electrical and chemical impulses required to sustain life. Through experiences, we learn to use the body better and more adeptly each day, from random movement of arms and legs to more controlled use of limbs and digits and senses. We literally learn mobility. We learn to see. We learn to hear. We learn to taste and touch and smell. We learn what the impulses that these senses bring to our brains mean. We learn to discern. We learn which signals are good (life sustaining) and which signals are bad (life threatening), and we do so with the help of humans that were born before us. This helps!

So what does this have to do with programs? Well, because we take so long to mature, and because the brain/mind is obsessed with learning what is life sustaining vs. what is life threatening to us for so many years, we have the opportunity to learn that the things that we experience as bad or life threatening may not universally be so, and to learn that things we experience as good or life sustaining also may not universally be so.

Let me give you an example. One child is raised with two loving parents who joyfully and patiently care for it. The family is connected as a unit and the parents know and can anticipate the child's needs almost before the child expresses them. They know when the child is hungry and tired and when the child wants to play and learn and they accommodate the child accordingly. The child grows and blossoms in their care, learning how to use its biology and navigate the world with curiosity and safety.

Now let's say there is another child who has a loving mother, but a father who is angry and abusive. This is not an uncommon scenario in our world (and we could just as easily say a loving father and a mother who is angry and abusive). Even though the mother is loving and kind and connected, the father is angry and abusive and dangerous. This baby will learn that its father is life threatening and learn to navigate the world and the father in a way that minimizes the danger and threat in order to ensure its continued survival. In essence this child is literally programmed to believe, by experience, that father = bad. While the other child is programmed to believe that father = good. A program warps reality, through positive and negative experience, to be other than what it truly, objectively is, which is that every father is unique and we must continue to discern anew in each moment.

We basically learn how to navigate the world based on two things: pleasure and pain. Pleasure = good and pain = bad. We move toward pleasure and way from pain. We move toward positive emotions and experiences and away from negative or painful or scary ones. And so it is we are programmed from a very early age.

Pleasure can take many forms, including acceptance in the form of praise. Being accepted and liked is a positive experience and so we move toward it.

Pain can also take many forms, including teasing. Teasing and rejection are negative experiences, so we usually move away from them.

In both cases, we learn what = pleasure (acceptance) and what = pain (rejection).

Let's not get caught up on the words here, but on the energy and feelings behind them. We move toward good feelings: acceptance, praise, reward, encouragement, love. We move away from painful experiences: teasing, punishment, rejection, hate.

What is insidious about programs is that we most often don't even know they are running us because we learned our behaviors at such an early age that memories of them are vague or hard to access. Some people resort to hypnotherapy to discover and remember their early memories.

Programs can also be created by the mind in an attempt to explain the why of a painful or pleasurable event in order to predict and either avoid reliving the pain of it or recreate the pleasure of it in the future. Programs give events meaning and are often stories about them.

At its simplest, the process of creating programs is one of classical conditioning. This is how we humans become meaning-making mammals.

I was teased mercilessly in elementary school. I was called names and bullied for simply being who I was. I was a bit more effeminate and sensitive than other boys, and I was drawn to being friends with girls at an age when the sexes remained segregated. The teasing and bullying HURT. It was like I was being punished for something I didn't understand. What was I doing or how was I being that was resulting in this painful experience of teasing and bullying? My mind searched and observed for what was appropriate and acceptable behavior. How did the other boys behave such that they did not become the target of this pain? What behavior would help me to avoid the pain of teasing and bullying?

My reaction to the pain was to decide that effeminate/sensitive = pain = bad.

I learned to feel ashamed of who I authentically was as a child because it caused me pain.

It is important to note that at such an early age we are just naturally expressing the version of US the Universe created us to be. It was effortless being me and yet it was painful because some others didn't like the me I was being. So, I worked to become less effeminate and less sensitive to avoid the pain. I started to abandon pieces of the authentic ME and exchange them for a constructed version of me that others wanted me to be because it was more acceptable and less painful.

Some kids in a similar situation to mine go the other way, they withdraw or rebel completely against what is acceptable and become entirely unacceptable to those that cause them the pain; then they just endure the pain when it happens.

Another one I discovered was a deep, deep, old, insidious program that went something like, "Anyone you love deeply will abandon you, so DO NOT get too close or love fully." This affected all my relationships. When I felt like I was falling in love or getting too close, and therefore was vulnerable to abandonment, I would suddenly turn and run as far and as fast as I could. This all played out seemingly automatically. I would feel it start and say, "Oh no, it's happening again," but I seemed to have no choice about it. It seemed to happen to me. I later discovered when spelunking deep in the caverns of my mind and psyche that when my father died suddenly when I was eight, it felt to my undeveloped mind that he abandoned me. I loved him more than anything or anyone in the world. He was my hero. The pain of the loss was so great that I literally lost the memory of almost a year and a half of my life.

My mind, in order to protect me, made up the story that people I love will abandon me and this program silently guided my creation. What objectively happened was that there was a terrible accident—a plane crash—that took my father's life. Everything else was the meaning I made of it to protect myself from ever experiencing that level of pain again. My mind imprisoned me inside the program it created, keeping me from loving deeply and completely for many, many years.

In both examples of programs, the pain of an event followed by my mind's meaning or story of the event altered my behavior and full expression of ME and locked me away to protect me and to try and prevent or avoid similar painful experiences in the future. The programs became permanent behavioral adaptations to reality. This happened automatically and unconsciously. So much so that I thought the adaptations were me and that this is just how I was. I must have been born with a crack in the foundation of my being and I'd just have to live with it.

Programs are everywhere. We must find them and untangle them one at time. Sometimes it's easier to start with the big, obvious ones since they are, well, so big and obvious. Most often these are the programs formed by traumas in our lives or larger abuses that we suffered and adapted to. Or we can start with smaller, more recent ones that don't live in as deep a place in our being.

Programming is happening everywhere, every day, in every culture and family. Become aware of what makes others comfortable and what makes them uncomfortable. People take jabs at what makes them uncomfortable, or what makes them feel afraid or threatened. They praise behavior that is acceptable. This is how we train dogs and animals and it is apparently how we train people, too, programing them to abandon the unique and perfect version of themselves for a version others are more comfortable with. Beware that as you wake up you don't become the perpetrator. Programs are a powerful force that can either keep us small or help you rise into the YOU who will rock everyone's world.

I say, go ahead ROCK everyone's world and ROCK yours while you are at it. Life will be much more beautiful and exciting when you do! The Universe will celebrate you being YOU more fully in each moment that you choose YOU instead of allowing your programs to choose for you.

When you discover your programs, play with them, dialogue with them, and seek to fully understand how they are guiding your behavior and affecting the life you are creating.

PROGRAM EXERCISE

A program is a story we've told our self or a meaning we've constructed to understand an event or occurrence that alters our behavior and self-expression going forward. In this exercise, you will search your life, working from today all the way back to your birth—scan both forward and backward along the timeline—and ask your all-knowing self where you were programmed by pleasure or pain. What was praised or encouraged in your family, peer group, or place of worship? What was condemned or discouraged? How were you conditioned by those around you or by someone you respected?

Let the memories flow and write them down.

Particularly ask your all-knowing self to show you the programs about areas of your life that you are always working to "fix," but just can't seem to no matter how many books you read or seminars you go to. Most assuredly, a program lives there.

Remember, this is NOT an exercise for the mind. You cannot ask the thing that created programs to relieve you of them. This is an exercise for the Universe within you. It is an exercise for your instrument, which can connect to your all-knowing YOU whenever you need it. Let yourself be guided to programs. When you do, you will be guided perfectly to the ones that you are ready to bring forth into the light of consciousness and release.

The more programs you drag into the light and release, the freer you will be.

How will you know that you have released a program? For me, it was evident because certain types of events occurred that would normally have set me off, activated my emotions, and sent me into a state, yet didn't. Once the core program was cleared, I noticed that there would be no response to these events. It was remarkable and I would find myself saying, "Wow, that didn't even bother me." I was free of the program that had created the automatic response and so there wasn't one.

Ahhhhh. There really is no better feeling. Such is the evidence of our awakening.

BELIEFS

Beliefs are a threat to our becoming because they often keep us from questioning and challenging and seeking. They make us lazy because they make us feel that we have no need to explore or discover the truth or any explanation outside of the belief.

Religions are belief systems. Political parties are belief systems. Economic systems are belief systems. Each belief system tells us what is best or right or wrong. Beliefs tell us how to think and be and behave, so it is important to evaluate our beliefs carefully. When beliefs lead us to choose our thoughts, words, and actions without examination, we are not free. When we allow our beliefs to choose for us without challenging those choices, we rarely choose the US the universe created us to be. We choose sameness. We fail to question.

Spontaneity and inspiration often lead to ideas and behavior that contradict our beliefs. Unfortunately, a mind governed by unexamined beliefs has very little room in it for inspiration or spontaneity. Beliefs are like walls that keep the Universe out, that keep us from discovering the truth that is uniquely our own and that is based on our own exploration of reality.

During the writing of this book, I came up against all kinds of fears, patterns, programs, and beliefs that became activated and tried to stop me. Some were beliefs I thought I'd addressed and released previously, and others were new ones that I had yet to discover. Surprise! I wrote two chapters of the book before my mind reared up and grabbed hold of me. I'm not sure why it allowed me to do those two chapters before jumping in, but in

BELIEF EXERCISE

Identify your beliefs and write them down. Start with big, easy ones, like the beliefs that go with your political party affiliation or religion or economic system. These are easy. Then work your way down to smaller or subtler ones by asking, "What do I believe about _____?" and filling in the blank.

Examine each of the beliefs. Ask yourself, "Do I know for certain that this is objectively true in the world without question?" If someone else believes something different as strongly as you believe what you believe, then the answer is NO, because saying yes would make you right and them wrong and objective truths are indisputable facts.

Become conscious of when your beliefs are choosing for you. Challenge your beliefs. Bring them into the light and then either choose them because they help you come home to YOU or discard them because they are obstacles to being and expressing authentically as YOU.

hindsight I guess it's because it didn't really take me seriously until the first two chapters flowed out and were actually, in my humble opinion, quite good! That was SCARY to my mind as it revealed a seemingly infinite landscape of possibilities and unknowns—and how could it protect me from what it didn't know? So my mind freaked out, panicked, and started throwing challenges at me things, like, "Who are you to write a book? What do you have to say that anyone wants to read? Why even try because you'll just quit anyway? You've never written a book, what do you know about it?" And on and on and on. . . . Punch, BIFF, POW, WHAM. I was taking hits from every angle. And it worked. I believed what my mind was selling and I quit. I quit because when I quit it told me I was safe and it felt like we (my mind and I) were safe.

I decided to go California to spend the winter away from Madison, Wisconsin. I landed in Santa Barbara where I have close friends and family. My amazing friend Tippy and her amazing husband, Tom, graciously let me take up residence in the guest house in their barn. I woke up every day to two beautiful horses, and sunny 70-degree days, and my dog, Max, was free to run and play safely in a big, beautiful yard. Life was perfect. But despite how perfect everything in my life seemed on every level, including the levels of health, work, finances, family, and friends, unexplainably I sank into the deepest and darkest depression of my life. It took everything I could just to get through each day and put a smile in front of the depression so I didn't worry anyone.

The difference this time was that I was awake inside my depression. I talked to it and I talked to the Universe. I did not let my depression overtake me and sleep-create my life. It took every ounce of energy and effort I had every day, but I pushed forward and put one foot in front of the other, so I didn't become the victim of my depression but a witness to it. I used all my tools. I asked the Universe to show me whatever it was that I needed to see and work through to get to the other side.

I said both to myself and the Universe, *How can it be that I've spent thirty years searching, letting go, releasing, overcoming, unlearning, and reprogramming my mind, and yet here I am in this place AGAIN?!*

When the answer came, which it did, I was too busy having my expectations about how I thought it would or should look to see it for what it was. That was because the answer challenged a powerful belief that I wasn't even aware was choosing for me. Even so, there was something different about the experience of my depression this time. This time it felt final, like a gateway—to what I did not know, however. Was it a gateway out or was it a gateway through?

Sometimes the mind holds so strongly to its fears, patterns, programs, and beliefs that it would rather we literally die than to release them and step into the vast unknown where it feels it cannot protect us and keep us safe. For me, this was one of those times. I was on the verge of jumping into a bottomless chasm of the unknown of putting myself out there, telling my story, and believing that what I'd learned and discovered on my journey might help others come home and remember. I hoped that *Potentialized,* the book, might be the ideal vehicle for me to do so.

The intensity of the depression grew and grew until I just couldn't take it anymore. Finally, one day, I screamed, "*WHAT AM I NOT GETTING HERE UNIVERSE? WHAT AM I NOT SEEING? WHY IS NO ANSWER COMING? WHY ARE YOU NOT SHOWING ME WHAT I NEED TO MOVE THROUGH THIS?*" Literally the same day, I got a call from my doctor whom I had recently seen for my annual checkup and who had actually saved my life ten years before. I had told her about the depression during my visit some weeks back, but since she was not the kind of doctor that dealt with depression, there was not much she could do. Unknown to me, however, she didn't let it go. Between my appointment weeks before and that day, she had taken it upon herself to find someone that she then insisted I see. Like the insisting she had done ten years before that saved my life.

This doctor friend sent me to see someone who was a psychiatrist, and not just a psychiatrist, but also a psychopharmacologist. Because I was literally at the end of my rope this day, hanging on by my fingernails, and because I screamed at the Universe to show me what I was not getting, I said I would go. But I did not intend to do ANYTHING this doctor recommended because I held the belief that psycho-pharmacology, and indeed almost all of western medicine, was corrupt and evil and addicted to, and perpetuating, disease in order for it to survive and profit.

After all, I was a good spiritual seeker! If I couldn't heal myself, mind, body, and spirit, naturally, well, then I was a failure. It would mean I had no business on this path. This was my belief.

I reluctantly went to see this doctor. He was semiretired; he never wanted to fully retire because he loved his work. He loved bringing people back into balance with themselves using the latest advances and medicines. I walked heavily into his office and sat down in a chair. (There was no couch as I'd imagined in my mind—a cliché, but true.) He asked me to fill out a rather lengthy questionnaire that was full of weird questions, like "Do you snore?" BOY, do I snore. But it was strange that he would ask that. *Doesn't he want to hear my story? Doesn't he want to talk to me about me?* I thought.

Once I finished the questionnaire, I handed it to him and he looked it over page by page. When he looked up, he said, "You've come to the right place. I can help you." *But how is this possible,* I thought, *considering we haven't said more than a few introductory words to each other?* I asked if he wanted me to provide any details about what I was feeling or what I was going through, and he said, "No, I'm not interested in your story. It is irrelevant. Your brain is an organ like any other and right now yours is out of balance and you are suffering. My only concern now is bringing it back into balance and relieving your suffering, and talking is not going to do that. I'm sure you've talked about all that's going on plenty. Has it helped?" I had to admit that it hadn't.

Then the doctor uttered the words that made me go against one of my MOST POWERFUL beliefs. He said "I am 100 percent confident that if you give me four to six weeks I can reacquaint you with the best version of yourself."

How was he so sure? He didn't know me. It was his confidence and kindness (along with my latest tantrum directed at the Universe) that made me say, "What the hell, I'll give you six weeks. I've got nothing to lose."

He wrote a prescription, I went to the pharmacy, and that's how I started my six-week adventure. And it worked. In six weeks, I was myself again. I felt balanced and whole and hopeful. I was not a disconnected, mindless, numbed-out version of myself that I was sure I'd be if I took medication. I was confidently and most assuredly ME.

This was not the sum total of the gift I received, although it would have been enough. I forced myself to sit within the realization that my mind (through the belief it held) would rather have seen me dead than let go of the belief that taking medication was wrong. Luckily this happened at a point in my awakening when I could remain conscious inside of the depression and not be fused with it. AND of course it happened at this perfect point, because the Universe NEVER gives us more than we can handle and she knows when we are ready.

I sat in this place for weeks and witnessed and observed and pondered. At the end I said to my mind, *I am DONE with this. I am DONE with you lying to me and telling me what I should do or what I cannot or should not do. I'm DONE with you scaring me into remaining small. I'm DONE with the stories that you use to imprison me. NO MORE! THAT'S IT! You would have rather I die than let go of a belief and step into the unknown because it is not safe. Well, I'm done with being safe. I'm done playing small. I'm done rattling around in this cage.* I declared myself free, I emancipated myself from the prison of my mind, and I admitted that I did not know ANYTHING about ANYTHING because I cannot trust what is real vs. what is a fabrication of my mind. I said to myself, *I DON'T KNOW. I will not pretend that I do anymore, and I will not let my mind pretend that it does ANYMORE.*

For the first time in my life, I had achieved the experience of not knowing and not trying to know. Without my mind to explain and make sense of my experience to me, I felt adrift in a vast, infinite void. I was rudderless and had no mind to provide stability and perspective. It felt like I would drown. It was terrifying and electrifying. It was what the mind had been most afraid of: not being needed. And just as I felt that I would drift and spin and fall, and perhaps be unable to function in the world ever again, I landed in the loving arms of the Universe, who softly said, "Congratulations, welcome home! I've got you and you are safe! I've always had you—look back and you will see. The flow that is the music of our dance has always existed between us though you have only been able to experience it sporadically because but all your focus was through the mind. A mind doing its very best, but a mind governed by fears, patterns, programs, and beliefs that have clouded and obstructed our connection until now."

Today, I swim and play in the flow. I live here. Any significant action I take is informed by my connection to the Universe. I am patient. I allow things their time. I do not push or pull or struggle anymore because I trust with every fiber of my being that the

Universe has me. She loves me and she knows me. She knows where I need to go, what I need to do, who I need to do it with, and when. It is the most beautiful dance I have ever danced. And it usually doesn't look like I "think" it would or should, but I trust her anyway. What I discover on the other side of leaping yet again into the void whenever she says, "Leap," is always more perfect than I ever could have created or imagined by myself and from my limited human perspective.

Once I merged with the flow, I only wanted one thing: whatever the Universe wanted for me. I ask only to serve her with all my gifts and my whole being, and I give her the gift of ME every day so that she may guide me, deploy me, instruct me, and use me to do Her bidding and help each of us come home to ourselves and find her within.

Until we recognize and experience that our mind uses fears, patterns, programs, and beliefs as ways to inhibit our expression, it will keep us trapped and imprisoned, and very little will be possible for us except what it creates and recreates for us. When these constructs are running our lives there is very little room for the Universe to conspire, inspire, co-create, expand, and become through us.

The force of the Universe in you that is seeking to express itself uniquely through you as YOU is the most powerful force in existence. The longer you try to hold the Universe down, keep her small, contain her brilliance, contain YOUR brilliance, the more painful living will become. So do your best every day to let go of one fear, one pattern, one program, one belief.

If you feel afraid or uncomfortable in this process, GOOD, you are on the right path. Just breathe, let go, and then take another step forward—and then another. You can never let go too much because you can never let go beyond the flow of All That Is. Be courageous. In this way, you will slowly become freer, more buoyant, more agile, and more adaptable to the spontaneity and flow of the Universe. With each release, you will feel lighter and the Universe will reward you with ease and joy and miracles and synchronicities.

I have a demand that I make of the universe often, which

goes something like this: "Universe, support me in being and be-coming the ME you created me to be every day. Help me express and celebrate ME better in every moment. Help me let go of any fears, patterns, programs, or beliefs that inhibit my authentic expression of ME. I am ready!"

Try it, but don't have an expectation of how the results will look or what fear, pattern, program, or belief you will be called upon to work through when you do. Ask it, demand it, and then let go. Just do your best to be ready, in every moment to meet her guidance and any opportunity the Universe presents to you.

Do this, achieve this, and your healing and remembering and expansion and expression of YOU will be supercharged. It will happen faster than you could ever hope for and yet at the perfect divine pace for YOU. And you might want to hold on, because it's an exhilarating ride.

CHAPTER SEVEN

LEARNING TO LISTEN

Having a conversation with the Universe
is an embodied experience
that requires your entire instrument.

The Universe is always communicating with us. This means that any answer to any question is there for you if you know how to listen to her voice. And yes, you do know how to speak her language, even if you don't think you do or remember how. We are born with this ability and it never goes away. "Hardwired" into each of our bodies is a system for direct communication with the Universe. She speaks to us through feeling, intuition, small miracles, synchronicities, and inner knowing.

To hear the Universe, you must listen with your whole body as a receiving instrument. She will speak to you and through you, but only when you remember how to perceive her subtle language.

By the way, she also hears everything we say. Lord knows I've yelled at her in anger, cried out in pain, spoken to her with soft gratitude, and even shared my tears of joy for the miracles she has conspired to deliver to me. I love conversing with her when I'm surrounded by nature, as in this setting it feels as if everything living thing around me is part of the conversation. But I've found she responds best when I speak to her like I'm talking to my best friend or someone I love, trust, and respect deeply—someone that is my equal. She does not require or appreciate subjugation. It is unnecessary as she sees everything in her creation as her equal.

Sometimes when I am asked to perform a particularly daunting task, like writing this book, I say, "Yes, of course," and acquiesce to her because I don't want her to escalate her request to a demand or knock me off my feet; I let her know in no uncertain terms that I will do it, but I respond that I will not do it alone. I tell her that her guidance and assistance and active support are required.

I have learned that I cannot do things alone, nor do I want my brain to struggle me through the "how to" of something I've never done. It's cute to watch it struggle and try to figure it out, but why put it or me through that when the all-knowing Universe will happily copilot the effort and provide just what I need when I need it, if I only ask?

The chatter of the mind is a noise that drowns out the voice of the Universe. If we want to hear her, we must learn to quiet the mind and come into right relation with it. Sometimes this will feel nearly impossible, such as when the child inside us is throwing a tantrum or the beast is roaring ferociously. But always, always, she speaks to us, ALWAYS!

Sometimes the Universe whispers to us almost inaudibly. She hopes we will hear her whispers, which are soft and cool like a summer breeze on your wet cheek. Over and over she will whisper her guidance lovingly and patiently, day after day, and we will hear it even though we may have to cock our heads to catch the tail end of the message, right before it loses its form and returns from whence it came. These whispers come like repetitive thoughts that we hear over and over again. Our mind will discard them—especially if it disagrees with them—and sometimes we think they are simply the ramblings of a mind lost in thought. But we can recognize the whispers for what they are, we can distinguish them from mental ramblings, because rarely, if ever, does the mind repeat itself softly in the background of its own chatter. It normally likes to think loudly, obsess, argue, ponder, and be busy-busy-busy all the live long day.

I have learned to hear the subtle, gentle whisper of the Universe, but only after time and again falling into sleep-creation mode and listening to nothing but the loud chattering commentary of my mind: Worrying about this, preparing for that, planning this, fearing that. All of it interfering with her insight. Our minds go on and on, telling us we are not worthy or good looking enough or smart enough, and we fall prey to those unfriendly messages, which drown out the loving voice of the Universe guiding us forward toward our highest potential.

Whenever my mind drowns out her voice for any extended period of time or if I simply fail to hear her quiet guidance, I notice that the Universe speaks more loudly. When whispering fails, she will up her game and start to nudge me in the ribs and raise her voice to get my attention. I've learned all too many times—the *hard way*—that it really is best to pay closer attention at this stage and listen to her not-so-gentle guidance.

Review your life. You'll remember where you yourself have experienced this. Each of us has missed a choice point or an off ramp from the mental superhighway that we kick ourselves for not taking in hindsight. Did you ever override a hunch or ignore a subtle warning signal and then wish you hadn't? Usually the experience we remember is painful enough that it jumps right out at us. If you look back, you'll likely see that you actually did hear the warnings, but were too stubborn or strong willed to heed them, or in denial because your mind convinced you not to believe the advice you were getting. The mind LOVES to debate the guidance of the Universe and it loves to WIN and be right. When you catch your mind debating an emergent thought, you can be sure that it is debating the guidance of the Universe because the mind usually does not introduce a thought just to debate itself. So pay attention or pay the price.

One time, an experience of ignoring the Universe was particularly painful, so much so that after the experience I swore I would listen ever more closely in the future.

It was February 2000 and I was working in New York City. I had a job in sales that I had grown disenchanted with; I had started not to believe in what I was selling, so I felt manipulative and dirty for getting out there and pretending that what I was selling was the best thing EVER and that anyone would be stupid not to buy it. Over and over I prayed for the Universe to bring me the perfect divine new job. It was time and I was ready. And she did. . . .

One day, I was in the shower and I literally heard a booming voice say, "Apply for X job at X company." I even remember looking up and thinking, *What was that?* And then I did what most of us do and started THINKING about it. For once my brain actually agreed with the guidance and saw how this highly coveted job as vice president of communications at an up-and-coming fashion company was within my grasp. It was magical how it occurred. The timing was perfect. I had the perfect relationships with the perfect people who recommended me for the perfect job and I got it . . . though, on the flip side, in my excitement at having heard the BOOMING voice that demanded action, I missed the Universe's follow-up whisper. I wasn't yet used to getting TWO significant communications in such a short period.

After I got hired into my new position, I heard the voice whisper, "Wait until Monday to quit your current job." In answer to which, the stubborn, bratty boy in my head said, *Why? Why do I have to wait? I want to quit now! I want out!* This time the mind won and I waited a day or so—but only until Friday—and then went into my boss Linda's office. Linda was amazing. I absolutely adored her and she was so patient with Bratty Brad. I went in, still shushing the voice that was telling me, "WAIT, WAIT, WAIT until Monday!" and I told her about the opportunity I had.

Linda took it well. She embraced me and remarked that it was a perfect opportunity for me and wished me the very best. "It has been a wonderful pleasure working with you," she said.

I felt so light and good. The whole thing had gone perfectly. Then Linda said she'd like to wait until Monday to tell the rest of the staff. Morale was low, she said, and it just didn't feel right to do it on a Friday afternoon.

Of course I agreed, and said, "Sure, whatever you think is best." Before day's end, a notice hit all of our inboxes saying to meet in the main conference room on Monday morning for an announcement. *Wow,* I thought, *an all-staff meeting just for me?*

I had a wonderful weekend. I was excited for a new chapter to begin in my career and very pleased that the boss I respected and adored so much had given me her blessing.

Monday morning came and the whole magazine convened in the main conference room. Except that when I arrived I saw that the CEO, Creative Director, and President of the company were there, as well as employees and representatives beyond my department. I quickly realized this meeting was not for me. Something bigger was happening. An important announcement was being made that would impact everybody.

That day, that very MONDAY, the company shut down our division. We were told that we had two weeks to gather our things, meet with Human Resources, and vacate the premises. There might be some positions in other divisions for some people, but for the most part a division of probably about sixty people was now out of work.

I felt stunned and lucky and guilty because of the new job that was in the bag for me. Then I discovered why the voice had demanded I wait until Monday. When I went in to meet with HR, they told me they had already been notified of my resignation on Friday. Had I waited until Monday, I would have gotten a severance check for $12,000, and instead of that, I got a "Congratulations and thanks for all your hard work."

OUCH!

This one hurt. While I felt lucky that I was literally one of the ONLY people that had a job to go to before the management shut us down, I was incredibly pissed at myself for not listening to the voice that had NEVER steered me wrong before and at my mind for talking me out of it. I had to swallow the big, dry, painful, golf ball-sized horse pill that my stubbornness had served up and that had cost me the perfect exit of a great job AND a good-sized severance. Not for nothing, that day I apologized to Spirit and thanked her for having my best interest at heart. Then I swore I would never ignore her urgings again.

It was a painful lesson and a turning point for me, but of course I would go on to do it again AND again because I am a silly, silly human.

One good way I have learned to listen for the voice of the Universe is to use music to help me bypass my noisy mind.

Have you ever noticed how sometimes you catch a tune in the distance or one comes on the radio and it literally moves you? Without thinking, your toe starts tapping or your hand starts slapping your knee? Or you just close your eyes and enjoy being bathed by a song's beauty? This is similar to how I "hear" the voice of the Universe speaking. I feel it—the message—before I am interrupted by thought. It is an impulse or an inspiration or an AHA or even a phrase or a thought repeated over and over throughout the day.

And what do we typically do with such messages? Our minds jump in and analyze and rationalize them and they shut that shit down. Just like when it catches us getting a little too funky to the tune that found our ears, it shuts us down. It says, "Hey, what are you doing? Someone might see you and you will look silly or crazy or whatever." And we stop.

Well, some of us do, and at some point most of us have.

If it helps you, like it helped me, use music to simulate the experience of listening to the voice of Spirit. But don't just listen to the music, feel it, let it get inside you. Let it take you on a ride. Let it dance your body. This is what having a conversation with the Universe feels like; it is an embodied experience that requires your entire instrument. It will feel like a dance. It will give you chills. It will send energy through your entire instrument. It will feel like you are in the groove or in the flow of something within and around us.

And when mind chimes in, and it will (mine still does), just ask it politely to sit down and shut up because you are getting your groove on with the Universe. Despite the pesky chatter of the pesky mind that keeps trying to shut it down or drown it out, you're learning how to listen to the special voice that is always speaking, whispering, shouting to get your attention and guide you.

With practice, you will get good at getting your groove on to the symphonic tune of the Universe communicating with you in every moment.

CHAPTER EIGHT

SAVE THE WORLD?

*Remember who you are—a snowflake-like soul,
unique and singular and true,
come to play in OUR creation.*

Once we are awakened creators, bravely advantaging ourselves of the opportunities for transformation and change in every new moment by choosing the thoughts, words, and actions that will help us realize the potential we were born to realize, what do we do? We save the world! We make it a better place. We live consciously. We recycle. We eat organic food. We spend time in nature. We do yoga. We meditate. We pray for peace. We drive hybrid cars. We urge others to do the same. We march. We condemn violence. We rage against the machine that enslaves us. We become vegans. We become Democrats or Independents or Green Party members. We say "Namaste."

We enshroud ourselves in a cloak of awakened smugness and self-righteousness. Because we are awakened, *dammit.* Our eyes are open, and dammit, everyone else is messing up our world: Polluting it. Starting senseless wars. Filling our oceans with plastic and chemicals. Poisoning our food supply. Buying our governments. Enslaving our people (those darn Reptilians). We become as righteous and indignant in our becoming and awakening as members of the Religious Right are about abortion or gay marriage, or as ISIS and the Taliban are about punishing the infidels of the West.

I am not judging. Oh no, I dare not! I am simply recalling who I became in the first few years after I "awakened" and who I've witnessed countless others become. I was nearly impossible to be around. So full of my own knowing. So sure that I was right and others were wrong. I was awake and others were asleep.

Because of my superior attitude I became part of the problem instead of part of the solution. I struggled with myself. With my family. With my friends. With my culture. With my country. I traded my own self-imposed struggles against my own becoming with struggles just as powerful against all that was out of alignment in our world because I could SEE it now. My eyes were open. I felt guilty that I had contributed to the pollution and the injustices so I did everything I could to tread more lightly while running around like a banshee telling everyone else (whether they wanted to hear it or not) that they were doing it "wrong." They needed to wake up!

I was not fun. Life was not fun.

Being self-righteous is lonely. Being right is lonely. You either find yourself hanging with other self-righteous, right people, who are arguing and screaming and making demands alongside you, or you find yourself alone because nobody can stand being around you. For me it was the latter. I was buckling under the weight of my self-imposed burden of saving the world from the human cancer that was destroying it.

This phase of righteousness is really another kind of sleep-creation.

Somewhere around this time of sleeping within my own awakening, the kind, loving Universe led me to explore the world of *entheogens*. Loosely defined, entheogens are natural substances, mostly of plant origin, ingested to produce nonordinary states of consciousness for spiritual purposes. The meaning, from the Greek roots, is "becoming Divine within." These are the medicines of indigenous peoples, of shamans, and they serve to connect you to YOU, to the Earth, and to the Universe, the creator of All That Is, Was, and Will Be.

When you take an entheogen, it gives you the embodied experience of unity, of oneness with all things big and small. They show you that you are entirely significant as creator, and yet utterly insignificant as a mammal on a tiny speck of dust in an infinite Universe. They crack you open and expose YOU to you.

To convey the impact and significance and power of their healing abilities is nearly impossible if you have not experienced them for yourself.

I am not advocating that you run out and partake of medicinal plants and substances. I was guided to them. When and if you are ready to try entheogens, you will be guided to them too or they will find you. Yet, just like the books I read and seminars I attended, it was up to me to integrate these powerful experiences and ultimately to change the way I thought, spoke, and acted so that I could align ever more deeply with the Creator within me and all things.

I could write an entire book on entheogens, but why would I? So many wonderful books and blogs and movies already have been written and filmed espousing their powers and gifts for transforming and awakening humanity. I only mention them here because they led me to an experience that forever changed me by relieving me of my self-imposed burden to save the whole wide world and the judgment that other's needed to wake up and get with the program. It is my personal belief that entheogens are part of the Earth's immune system helping to awaken humanity to our connection to each other and her before the cancer we are consumes her. (Although to be frank, I suspect she may have some other tricks up her sleeve if these substances fail to get the job done, and I don't think it'll be pretty if she has to pull out these big guns.)

It was in 2010 or 2011 or 2012 . . . I really can't specifically recall the date . . . and anyhow, the year is irrelevant to the story. I was at a spiritual retreat in the Berkshires of Western Massachusetts with a group of fellow *entheonauts* (people ready to blast off into inner space). We were in sacred ceremony with a teacher plant and exploring the woods. I broke off from the group and soon found myself atop the root ball of a fallen tree. This root ball must have been between six and eight feet in diameter. I observed the swaying of the forest as it was breathing and dancing. I felt the cool breeze caress my face and body. From my perch, the sun illuminated and warmed the depths of my being. Clouds rushed by and I observed them without thought.

I felt as if I was the eye of Universe taking in the beauty and perfection of my creation, proud, ecstatic, and in awe of the miracle of it all. All the creatures and beings that collaborated daily to create and recreate everything my eyes could see were dancing together, each contributing its own unique purpose to the balance of the whole. Effortlessly. By design. I began to dance with them. Swaying gently at first, and then it came, the booming, beautiful sound of the symphony of life.

This wasn't a sound I could hear with my ears, like the "voice" that speaks to me as the Universe. To hear it, I had to listen with my whole instrument, both corporal and etheric.

I picked up my invisible conductor baton and I conducted the silent symphony of the Earth. It must have gone on for an hour. I had chills over my entire body. I laughed. I cried (more sobbed). I smiled a knowing and grateful smile. I remembered. I looked down and saw craggy roots protruding from rocky soil. The roots of the fallen tree were reaching, longing. The tree, though fallen, was still alive. The tenacity of it. The audacity of it. I was overcome with sadness suddenly at what humanity was doing to Mother Earth. This benevolent, loving being that literally provides the matter our souls inhabit during this lifetime, this adventure. And we repay her by desecrating her! Polluting her. Senselessly killing her creatures and destroying her delicate ecosystems. Living amok without gratitude. I cried and cried and cried because I saw how the human organism that was created to participate and contribute and collaborate in Earth's creation, like all the other living creatures, in perfect balance and harmony, had become like a cancer on her body that ravaged and destroyed.

I grabbed hold of the roots and sent her my deepest apologies—from my soul to hers. Suddenly, I was taken on what seemed like a roller-coaster ride. She showed me her beauty and our ugliness. She showed me the faces of children laughing and of children suffering. She showed me plastic and war and deforestation and high-fructose corn syrup and GMOs and the Pacific gyre—a vortex of plastic and metal trash caught in the ocean current. She also showed me waterfalls and rainbows and violent storms and gentle breezes. It went on and on. At the end of this journey, I apologized again and cried and cried some more.

Like any good human sincerely and authentically apologizing for his wrongs, I expected to be forgiven and given instructions on how to do better. Be better. Instead she interrupted me mid apology and with great power and grace exclaimed: "I do not need or require your apology. You have done nothing to apologize for. I gave you life on my body on purpose. I gave humanity permission to be and become exactly who and what you are without exception. You are beautiful and perfect and we are in this dance together you and I. I take full responsibility for my creation.

"I've got this. I can handle plastic and war. I can repopulate the species that are dying with new wondrous creations, as I have before. I can right the perceived imbalance at any moment of my choosing, as I have before. And like you, I can pass into death with grace and ease if that is my choosing and it is my time. All of it perfect. All of it divine.

"So relieve yourself of this burden of worry that you are doing this to me. I chose this. I created this, and I take responsibility for my creation. Period. If you want to show me your gratitude for the body and life I have provided you freely, and for the experience of living on my body then I ask only that you live fully. Recognize and remember who you are—a snowflake-like soul, unique and singular and true, come to play in OUR creation. Contribute your singular note and frequency fully and confidently to the silent symphony of creation that you were so beautifully conducting only minutes ago.

"Take care of yourself. Take full responsibility for your creation. Heal yourself. Heal your thoughts and words and actions, and through this all will move toward balance and healing. You have the opportunity to rise fully into yourself and I invite you to do so. Come home to yourself. To the YOU that WE created you to be. Do this and I will weep with joy, for it is all I want of any of my creatures. I want them to fully express their purpose and potential always and in all ways."

The love I felt from the Earth seemed to permeate every cell of my being. So deep was this love. So true and unwavering. So powerful and so gentle. *Unconditional* doesn't even begin to describe it. It was infinite and limitless, and it fundamentally changed me. My journey and approach to living was forever altered.

Although the Earth relieved me of the burden to "save the world," or some small and particular part of it, I realized that when we truly awaken to our purpose and potential we naturally contribute to the rebalancing and healing of humanity and the Earth. It must be so. Because if the purpose and passion you remember or discover is about elephants and wanting to ensure that they are revered and protected, then this is your note to play in the symphony of creation. If your passion and purpose is to ensure that gay men and women have the same rights as any other human then you'll take your case to the Supreme Court at the perfect moment, and evolution and change will be the result. If the dance you remember to be your authentic dance takes you to the rainforest where you bask in Earth's beauty and pledge your heart and soul to protect her, then the Universe has called you forth to serve HER in this way.

When we follow an inner calling it cannot help blossoming within us because it is US. When we are aligned with ourselves our healing is HER healing. It cannot *not* be so.

When we simply express our passion and purpose fully and give all of ourselves toward this end, then fundamental transformation on all levels is not only possible because it happens on the cellular level within the organism we call Earth, it is also inevitable.

If you are not sure what your purpose is or how you can serve, ask the Universe. She will tell you. I trust her with my whole being without question or reservation.

CHAPTER NINE

DON'T TRY THIS ALONE

The answers we seek to all the prayers we pray
lay within the collective organism that is humanity.

There is no more powerful way to heal the world than by engaging in the selfish act of self-expression. If you are not busy saving the world, then you are free to simply shine the radiance of YOU everywhere you go. Wherever you are, whenever you are, whatever you are, however you are—there YOU are! But there is one more teensy-weensy principle that the Universe lovingly whacked me over my stubborn head with after she saw me pushing and struggling and willing my way forward, trying to go it alone. I was utterly convinced I did not need anyone or anything but me, my dog, and my relationship to nature and the Universe to do whatever needed to be done.

In hindsight, I'm sure that the Universe and all her angel buddies sat around up there in no-time, no-place enjoying their vanilla soy half caff lattes and assorted baked goods, and having quite a laugh at my expense while watching me stubbornly, insistently declare, "I got this. I can do it by myself." Yep, they let me wrestle and go it alone for a good long time until they grew bored and she finally interrupted me. (Of course, by then I was red faced, sweating, and exhausted).

The Universe said, "*Pssst.* Yo Bradley, silly human, come here. Sit down and have a listen. I created seven-plus billion of you, and well, *uhm,* the point is that you aren't supposed to do it alone. Yeah, seven-plus billion points to be exact. So, might I ever-so-kindly suggest that you ask for help? And allow others the gift of helping you? Might you try calling others forth to be and express perfectly who and what they were created to be, and put it in service to you and your efforts? This is how it is supposed to work.

"You need each other, Bradley. I couldn't possibly put all the tools needed for living on this complex planet and in your complex human society in your tool chest. You couldn't lug that thing around, it would be so heavy. And it would blow your mind, literally, so I split up the infinite gifts and tools needed for this adventure and sprinkled them across the whole of humanity. So stop trying to fix it yourself, change it yourself, do it yourself all by yourself. Sure, it's cute and fun for us to watch, and all, but you really are not getting anywhere this way because you keep slipping and falling in your own mess.

"When you pray to me for help and guidance and miracles, for new friends, new loves, new work opportunities, and for cures for whatever ails you, rest assured that I hid the answers to your prayers in the humans you encounter every day. Yes, the ones you walk by, judge, make fun of, laugh at, disregard, and otherwise ignore. Yep, them. So pull your head up. Look around you. And start looking for what you are praying for in your fellow humans. Look for it with more than your eyes. Use your heart and the intuitive knowing that allows us to speak these words to each other.

"When you've found the right solution, the right person, you will feel the connection and see the spark, and you will know who carries the gift I have sent forth in answer to your prayers. This is by design.

"And maybe this will interest you . . . the gift you may think is just for you is actually for you both, because you both receive a gift in the giving and receiving of it.

Stunned. Silence. DOH! Boy, did I feel stupid. I'd been going it alone for so many years trying to survive that I had forgotten there was any other way. I had forgotten that I needed to rely on myself, on the Universe, AND on my fellow humans to help me realize my dreams and answer my prayers. I looked back at all the prayers that had been asked and answered, and realized they were all answered through another person. Every single one. Whether it was the apartment I got in New York City, or a job, or a love . . . it was always another human being who made it possible.

And all the time I was suffering from the delusion of solo accomplishment and bragging to myself and others, "Look at what I did."

I was literally rolling on the floor, laughing my ass off, and peeing my pants a bit when I realized this. I never did it alone, EVER. And now I was aware of it, conscious of it, it felt AWESOME! I felt huge gratitude that the Universe was sufficiently tired of her latte and baked goods to come to me with one of her reality-shattering *Psssts.*

Love that woman!

It came to me on a recent plane trip that if, as we awaken, we do not fall deeply and unwaveringly in love with humanity—with all of humanity, the good and the bad, the beautiful and the ugly, the gentle and the forceful, the loving and the mean, the perfect and the imperfect of it, that we are slumbering still. Because the answers we seek to all the questions we can ask, all the prayers we pray, and all the tools and gifts we need to navigate and awaken to this reality lie within the collective organism that is humanity. So it is by design that we should not, and cannot, do it alone.

By seeking answers to our questions and prayers in others, we call upon them to claim their unique gifts and special knowing, and to express themselves in such a way that they give us a gift that nourishes their souls and our souls, and serves to awaken us to our perfect divine purpose and potential.

For God's sake, ask for help already! But don't ask anyone to carry you or your baggage . . . just ask them to share the gift and spark of knowing within them that the Universe so lovingly and magically sprinkled into all humanity so that we could awaken one another by giving each other just what we need, when we need it, and answering our prayers! We are the ones we've been waiting for! Truly.

CHAPTER TEN

THE RADICALS

*Lucid living takes great courage for the human,
but not for the soul.*

have committed myself to five tenets that I use to guide my life, my relationships, and my communication. I call them the Radicals.

- ▸ Radical courage
- ▸ Radical responsibility
- ▸ Radical forgiveness
- ▸ Radical honesty
- ▸ Radical self-care

The adjective *radical* adds force, focus, and amplification to whatever other word it precedes. It implies an essence that is fundamental and unwavering.

The Radicals are tools we can use to affect change in our fundamental nature. They reprogram us by shattering old fears, patterns, beliefs and programs, freeing us to create new possibilities. Like a rocket ship breaking free of the Earth's gravitational pull, the Radicals help us as individuals to break free of the gravitational pull of safety, shoulds, other people's opinions, stories, myths, and societal norms. We cannot break through to what is possible for us and be potentialized when we allow these limitations to continuously trap us in the orbit of mediocrity. Escape velocity takes a great deal of force in the form of bravery, honesty, deep love, and respect for self, absolute forgiveness on all levels, and most importantly, it requires clear and unfettered access to the deep and Universal drive and desire in all things to realize their highest purpose and potential.

The Earth germinated knowledge of the Radicals within me the day I danced on entheogens in the forest. As I started to use them in my life, my further awakening and transformation were catalyzed. In expressing them through me and sharing them with people I knew—friends and colleagues and clients—I catalyzed awakening and transformation in others, and I experienced how simple and powerful they are. They are gifts that give to all who touch and experience them, when they are used benevolently. So I share them with you now in the hope that they will help catalyze your awakening and transformation and do the same for those with whom you choose to share them.

There is no priority or order of importance to the Radicals, but they do seem to flow one into the other in an order unique to each individual who chooses to utilize them.

Use them wisely, use them kindly, use them selfishly and only for your own benefit and others will benefit by the experience and by association. Do not use them to teach or push or be right (though you probably will early on, as I did). Like a wizard mastering a new wand, you will have misfires. There will be collateral damage akin to turning one's friend into a toad or causing a hideous wart to appear on the nose of a foe. Luckily, the consequences of these misfires are temporary and we can alleviate their impact by being radically honest and taking radical responsibility for our errors.

How do I gauge this you might say? Well, first, if you are raising your voice or speaking down to someone or being rude …STOP! You are not coming from benevolence. You are coming from ego and you are looking to win or be right. STOP. Then try again later.

In such cases, refer to Chapter 13, "Help, I've Been Hijacked!" Use the tools you read there to find your center before you try again. But do try again. It's worth it.

Important: Do NOT beat yourself up or judge yourself for not knowing how to use the Radicals wand at first. It takes time and practice. You will misfire and there will be toads. So kiss the toads and forgive yourself, and try again. And by all means, admit what you are doing to those you turn into small woodland creatures.

"*Umm,* sorry, I'm practicing this new magic called the Radicals and I think I might have misfired all over you. My apologies. Send me the bill for the dry cleaning. . . ." Got it? Good.

When the Radicals are used correctly, there is NEVER a loser in the interaction or exchange, EVER. There are only win-win learnings and openings in which both parties experience relief, connection, remembering, awareness, and awakening, ALWAYS. This is not negotiable. No "buts" allowed. If you are hurting someone, stop. If you make a mess of your friendships and relationships because you abuse the Radicals and go around declaring your truth without invitation, and demanding agreement, do not blame it on me or the Radicals. Take responsibility for your misfire, reread this chapter, and ponder the use of these tools before trying again.

Lord knows, we don't need any more pain or suffering inflicted on us or on the world whether on purpose or unintentionally. If you create any messes, clean them up.

RADICAL COURAGE

I've always felt that it is a courageous soul that chooses to forget who it is and where it comes from in order to don an earth suit and adventure forth into creation to play, discover, feel, sense, and emote. Truly, this adventure requires no ordinary courage. It requires radical courage.

I cannot count how many times I've said to a friend who I know that I knew up there before here, or between trips, "Why, oh why, didn't someone stop me this time? Why did they let me do this AGAIN? Next time, BEFORE I strap on a baby human suit to start the ride, PLEASE pull me aside and show me the home movies from the last trip. And then torture me, burn me, drown me, waterboard me, pull out my fingernails with pliers, starve me, beat me, and ask me again if I really want to do this, cause this shit is HARD! For realz!"

At which point the Universe steps in, pushing my friend to the side, and responds the way she typically does, "GIRL, please! You begged to come back down here. You knew exactly what you were in for and you BEGGED to come! You were like a kid coming up on his annual trip to Disneyland. You barely slept or ate for decades in anticipation. You even tried to cut the line to get here sooner." She tells it like it is.

Then she continues, "The soul doesn't require courage to come here. Coming here makes it feel ALIVE, because here it can FEEL. At home in the realm of no-time there is only being, and the constant state of feeling is one of heightened ecstasy. You humans could not hold the energy of this state, although some of you try and some of you even get close. The enormity and vibration of it would blow your earth suit to pieces. It is beautiful and perfect and infinite—and yet it is only one of infinite levels of creation in our creation.

"A soul, once it has experienced the many facets of emotion and feeling and physical sensations that are available to it through the Earth experience, longs for more such experiences. It longs to discover new and different nuances of experience and feeling and physical sensation. As it swan dives into the ocean of possible human experiences, it knows that no matter what happens it will come home again. It knows that the sliver of reality that it temporarily occupies within the infinite spectrum of realities lives within All That Is so it never really left home in the first place.

"No, dear human, courage is not required for a soul to go forth and play in OUR creation, it longs for these adventures. Courage is only required for you to achieve what is ultimately possible in your realm! And that is for YOU to awaken and remember who YOU are and where you come from while alive inside the adventure. Up here, we call it *lucid living!*

"Lucid living takes great courage, but not for the soul. It takes great courage for the human."

The Universe is right about us. It is the human that slumbers, not the soul. It is the human side of us that gets caught in the gravitation pull of the stories and myths and judgments of our families and societies and cultures and religions. It is the human who allows its unique, brilliant, singular expression to become enshrouded in the black, pasteurized, homogenized goo that hardens into layer after layer of mediocrity and sameness over our radiance.

Fear not, however. Your radiance is never truly diminished. It is only hidden. No one can take YOU from you. The force that can emancipate your radiance from its gooey prison is, you guessed it, COURAGE. Radical courage!

Radical courage is needed to take responsibility for your creation—all of it, the good, bad, ugly, and beautiful. Radical courage is required if you are to forgive yourself and others completely and without restraint, and if you are to be radically honest knowing that in doing so you will give yourself and others the gift of permission to do the same, and if you finally are to put yourself first, make yourself a priority, and protect and care deeply for YOU.

You can be radically courageous starting right now. As with any of these new concepts, you can start small, try at first to simply say yes when you mean yes and no when you mean no and don't apologize if someone is displeased. This takes radical courage. You were born with all the strength and ability you need to awaken, be YOU, and live lucidly while alive inside this adventure. You've already begun. I know this because you are here!

RADICAL RESPONSIBILITY

Racial responsibility means owning your creation, right now, without exception, without apology, without judgment, without caveats, without excuses, without blame. This, your life and the state of it, is YOUR creation. No one else's. You did this, bad or good, beautiful or ugly, challenging or easy. You created it one thought, one word, one action at a time, making choices—either consciously or unconsciously—in every moment. The state of your life, health, finances, relationships, and profession are the sum total of the choices you have made through the thoughts, words, and actions you have chosen from the infinite options available to you in every moment.

Radical responsibility does not only apply to the past, radical responsibility is about the power of free will and conscious choice you have in every single moment of every single day. Right now, this moment, is a reset, a blank canvas, a new opportunity. You can choose whatever you want. Literally, you can choose

WHATEVER YOU WANT. Yet most of us CTRL C + CTRL V the last moment into the next and so we perpetuate a reality we pray to be liberated from.

You can choose to do nothing in this now moment or you can choose to take a walk or to go to the kitchen for a drink of water. While these types of choices may have very little impact on the trajectory of your life, you can also choose to take a risk in your relationships or work. You can leave a job that is not serving you, or leave a relationship that brings little joy. You can *carpe diem* ("seize the day") and call that person you have feelings for and tell him or her because you recognize that you have nothing to lose and everything to gain.

Radical responsibility means waking up to the fact that you are the chooser always, and there always is a choice. There is always a fork in the road, whether or not you perceive it, where you make a choice. When you know this, when you really get this fact, then you have to take radical responsibility for your past, present, AND future! When you get this, you realize that you have been your own jailer and only you hold the keys that will emancipate you from the prison of choices you have made. Unless, of course, you LOVE every choice and you love your life and health and relationships and work right now. If you love the status quo, then keep doing what you're doing!

OK, so I'm going to take it all the way and be radically honest about radical responsibility. No one can EVER make you do ANYTHING. You always have a choice. Even if you argue that choosing something means death or getting fired or losing everything, you still have a choice. And if you choose something, own the choice and blame NO ONE ELSE for the choice. This is radical responsibility. This is true liberation from being the victim regardless of the circumstances.

I'm not saying I'm there, that I've achieved this state in every situation for all time to come. But taken all the way to its extreme, this is radical responsibility.

Radical responsibility has been a hard one for me to master. Actually, all the Radicals were hard for me. I should have been banned for life from using my Radicals wand due to the number of times it has misfired on me. But slowly, experience after experience, I have become better at being radically responsible, and moved toward mastery of this tenet for how to approach life. I still have work to do on this Radical—and probably will until I draw my last breath.

At first, I railed against accepting responsibility for my state of unhappiness and my suffering. To me there were clearly causalities, people, and events to blame for my unhappiness. Right? I didn't choose for my father, my hero, who meant everything to me, to die in a plane crash when I was eight years old. The hurt scarred me deeply and the wounds festered as long as ten, twenty, and even thirty years later. And I didn't choose to be sexually abused before I was ten years old, in the process having my whole concept of sexuality and respect and love for men put into a blender and twisted and warped beyond recognition. Also I didn't choose to be teased or be beaten up for being different. And on and on and on, and blah blah blah.

No, I was correct: I did not choose these things. They happened. Death and abuse and cruelty are common occurrences in our perfectly imperfect world of broken humans banging around trying to figure IT out and awaken. I did not choose these experiences. But I did choose to believe *the stories I created around them*—even if I did so unconsciously. And I chose the thoughts, words, and actions that those stories gave rise to—each and every one.

Even if the stories were written by a young mind that could not possibly have understood the whys and wherefores of what had happened, I wrote the stories to explain these events to myself. I have to become conscious to the stories and take responsibility for writing each and every one if I am to be free.

And when I truly and deeply believed my stories and I held on to the "truth" of them so that I could make sense of reality. Even though these stories were warped and far from the truth, I am responsible for believing them for as long as I did. It's even hard to write that now, but I know that it is true.

Ironically, it was my desire for relief from suffering the consequences of the stories I created that sent me searching for answers, so in a way I am grateful for the pain of my stories. But they were just stories, including the story I made up about the experience of being molested and the story I made up about the experience of being teased.

I can see now that broken, imperfect humans who were doing the best they could in the moment they caused me harm and pain. But I made it about me. I decided there was something wrong with me rather than with them. Now I know that it wasn't about me at all. It was about them and their pain. Their behavior was related to the abuses they had suffered. Their separation of self from self, not mine.

That does not make it right and it does not mean I condone abuse or bullying in any way. But sticking to the objective facts liberates me. Taking radical responsibility for the creation of the stories I lived by transforms me from victim to awakened creator.

Despite our abuses and sufferings, we can love on, unbroken in spirit, mind, and body. Although some of us temporarily lose our way in the darkness of suffering, we can remember and awaken. When we take radical responsibility for the choices we make, including EVERY experience we have, we turn on the light.

It's a hard concept to embrace. I am not going to lie to you about that. But if you are able to take full responsibility for your creation—which requires you to view yourself as an aspect of the Universe creating in every moment—you will realize the power you have to create whatever you choose now. That power arising within you is the very same power that created the heavens and the Earth, and it is yours to master in any moment.

Another challenge I had with taking responsibility for my creation was that it required firing a large inner staff of pity party planners and PR professionals. Oh child, but could they throw and publicize a pity party! They loved me the victim. The less I took responsibility for my creation, the bigger a victim I was, and the bigger the victim I was, the bigger the pity party. And my PR gals, they could broadcast the pity party far and wide to ensure maximum attendance.

Of course, on the outside, this comes across like whining and complaining and "Can you believe . . . ?" and "That's so unfair!" Then all the fellow victims in our lives come running to join the complaining and whining and make us (and themselves by extension) right. They agree with us and validate the seeming truth that we have been egregiously wronged. And then we party on together with emotions popping and powing and zapping all over place. In this way, our stories are individually and collectively validated and strengthened.

It feels good to be right. To be validated. But it keeps you stuck in a cycle of victimhood that CTRL C + CTRL Vs your past right on into your future.

The only way out of this cycle is taking radical responsibility for your life, and of course, sending your staff of pity party planners and PR pros packing.

They don't go quietly, mind you—oh hell no! They "BUT THIS" and "YOU NEED ME" and "IT IS UNFAIR" all the way out the door. Even when you shut it and lock it, they peep through a cracked window and exclaim, "Life IS unfair" or "You need us," or some other such nonsense. The best thing to do is to thank them for their service, as they only did what you asked of them. Appreciate how much energy you gave them and then redirect that same amount of energy toward your own liberation and awakening from the fictitious stories you have written.

Silly, silly humans.

RADICAL FORGIVENESS

I discovered radical forgiveness later in the game, long after I'd already achieved it. It arrived like a sneak attack. A tap on your shoulder that says, "Oh yeah, and by the way, you did this and it was important, but if I had told you that you were doing it at the time you would have said, 'No way, I can't, I won't,' and you would have stopped."

Like I said, none of the Radicals is easy to practice. Remember it takes force to break free from the gravitational pull of our old patterns, programs, and beliefs. It feels good to blame and we often feel 100 percent justified in doing so. But if we don't make an effort, our blame keeps us earthbound or trapped in a low orbit far below the one where our divine potential lies. Far, far below it.

My dear friend Rebecca asked me to clarify radical forgiveness for her after I pointed out in an impromptu session of radical truth telling (before which I asked her permission to share with her what I was seeing and feeling) that her potential and future success were being significantly diminished by those she blamed for hurting and wronging her in the past. And let me tell you, like me she had every right to be MAD at those people and blame them for their mean-spirited and malicious actions.

As we were talking, an image of her presented itself to me: I saw her as a powerful winged she-warrior, ready and capable of going forth into the future and creating a life for herself that was better than her wildest imaginings. Yet I also saw something strange: There was a dark band, like a giant rubber band, wrapped around her heart. It reached back into the past behind her and was attached to experiences with two individuals who had caused her pain. The powerful she-warrior was unaware of being tethered to the past. It tried to take flight with its big beautiful, powerful wings, but was never able to do so because of the hold the past had on it—the anger and blame. In sharing this image, I was able to communicate the what and why of radical forgiveness.

Side note: The Universe speaks to us in many ways. Some people hear thoughts, some can speak the language of rocks or trees or animals. She loves to speak to me using images and often when I share these images the person I'm receiving them for "gets it" better than if I tried to verbally explain a concept. And as I've shared above, she also uses what translates to a voice in my head. Each of has our own way of perceiving and receiving the communications of the Universe. As you explore and deepen your connection to her, you will discover how your own instrument communicates with her.

OK, back to the topic at hand.

Radical forgiveness does not mean radical forgetfulness. It means that when we come to see and understand that whoever hurt us (however they hurt us, and whenever they hurt us) did so in their own potentialized state. In that moment (or those moments), they were doing the best they could, given their history, pains, abuses, neglect, and stories. MOST IMPORTANTLY, they are no longer hurting us. They hurt us in the PAST. So, in this moment it is we ourselves who are keeping those hurts alive by carrying them forward into the present and then into the future.

We do this, whereas they stopped hurting us at some point in the past. To stop being hurt, we must stop reviving the old hurts over and over again in our minds.

We can keep fanning the flames of that hurt every day through our blame and anger and by remaining a victim long after an incident has past—or we can forgive. If we fan the flames, it tethers us to the past and prevents us from moving forward. To truly forgive, for this reason, is ultimately a selfish act (radical self-care). We must do so in order to free ourselves from the illusion that we are still the victim of a person or an experience that no longer exists.

Think about this for a moment. We literally continue to be wounded by the memory of an experience and the story we created about it and NOT by the actual experience or perpetrator. In this way, we become our own victimizers. We keep the abuse alive day after day and week after week and month after month and year after year, and allow it to poison the present. Where is the abuser or perpetrator today? What are they doing? Are they thinking about you? Usually, I'd say 99 percent of the time the answer is no. You are the one keeping them in your life by remembering and reliving the abuse or event in the current moment.

For those currently in an abusive situation, I do not make light of your situation. I love you and I support you in choosing to get out.

If we can forgive the perpetrator of a hurt, forgive the act, forgive ourselves deeply and completely, we set ourselves free to take flight and create new, more wondrous realities that are not limited by a particular past event.

Forgive for you. But also know that in forgiving—truly forgiving—you not only allow yourself to heal, but the other to heal from the self-inflicted wounds and guilt they carry about the event that keeps them trapped in self-judgment and remorse and in the abuse cycle that they experienced.

When during a deep therapy session I remembered who in my life had perpetrated sexual acts on my nine-year-old boy self I did not feel anger. I felt relief. I had carried with me a dreamlike memory of a monster at the door of my childhood home. This disturbing memory was always with me. It was a nightmare that had seemingly occurred with such frequency that it burned itself into my memories. My therapist knew of this memory and she nonchalantly told me that we'd get to it when the time was right. One day, the time was right and the entire memory blew right open. I saw the face of the perpetrator and my world spun—literally, it spun—like when you have vertigo, and I thought I would pass out or throw up from the shock of the remembering. My therapist lovingly guided me through the disorienting sensation. She said, "Breathe and let it spin. You are reconciling realities. You are reconciling a story with truth." And so I spun, and then it stopped and I felt deep relief.

What I learned is that the abuse had happened because a man close to our family had taken advantage of me when I was longing for the comfort of "father" after my father died. What had started me spinning was the discovery that although the abuse was horrific and damaging enough to be enshrouded in a false memory of a monster at my door, I had to admit that something about the connection and the attention I got through the experience was pleasing to me.

That is radical honesty. Ouch! But it is true and it is OK.

Seeing the truth, I forgave the man and myself. I was genuinely grateful for getting clarity on a piece of programming that had made such a profound impact on my life and felt emancipated from a nightmare that until this point made no sense yet that impacted my life and relationships every day. And like my wonderful therapist so wisely understood, when I was ready, it was revealed and I healed.

I am in no way saying that my path of forgiveness without anger or need for justice is the high road or the better road or the right road. Each of us must choose how we want to deal with our own revelations of abuse or other violations and hurts in our lives in our own ways. If you feel a perpetrator of violence against you needs to be brought to justice and punished, then do so. It is your right. Just know that every day you carry forth the past experience into your future you are choosing to limit what is possible and delaying your healing.

The reason this guideline is called radical forgiveness is that it only considers what is best for YOU and what YOU need to create a better, more potentialized next moment. That's powerful stuff. And remember, radical forgiveness does not mean you forget—although you may gain such peace from it that you do forget. It does not mean you have to approve of, or love, or live with, or be friends with a person you are forgiving. But it can. We have seen stories where people befriend the murderers of their loved ones and discover miraculously deep levels of healing that would otherwise not have been possible. This is radical forgiveness at work, a gift for each in the giving of it.

We all have the ability and capacity to forgive fully and completely. We are God incarnate. And the God within us forgives completely and without exception all trespasses the very second after the trespass or abuse or pain or event has occurred. It is only the human and the mind that choose to hold on to pain, events, and trespasses. It is the human part of us that chooses not to forgive and instead to carry forward the pain, the wound, the hatred, or the judgment and to allow it to poison another day.

As I write this section, I have to acknowledge how hard it is to forgive. I hated and blamed for years. I blamed God for taking my father from me. I blamed my mother for, well, just about everything I could, but especially for not protecting me from the pains of life both remembered and hidden. I raged and blamed and believed I was right in doing so with all of my being. Until one day, while engulfed in all my rage and blame, during a morning walk with my dog, the Universe spoke softly to me and asked, "So how does all this rage and blame feel?"

Of course, I was a stubborn shit and responded, "GOOD!" to

which she responded "Really? Truly?"

I could have argued longer with her, but I have learned there is really no point. So I admitted that rage felt like poison in my being. I felt toxic and poisoned every day. The quality of my whole life was impacted. My thoughts were poisoned, my attitude was poisoned, my words were poisoned, and my actions were poisoned.

Then the Universe asked the simplest and most powerful of questions: "And what impact is all this rage and hate having on its target?"

Hearing this stopped me in my tracks. I didn't even have to ponder the question for a second to answer it. "NONE!" I declared.

DRAT!

I don't know why, but I had always thought my rage and hurt and anger were punishing the perpetrator, but she, my dear sweet mother, a woman who always only did her best, which in hindsight was pretty damn good, felt NOTHING. She was going about her day completely unaware of my self-imposed toxicity.

And this is when I first discovered—without yet naming it— radical forgiveness. Forgiving people for their crimes against me so that I could be free of the hold those crimes had on me every day was radical. At last I could be free from their poison, heal, and move on, leaving the past in the past and allowing myself to create new possibilities in the very next moment. Right on the spot, with only my dog to witness it, I forgave my mother. I saw the ridiculousness of me bashing myself in the head with the hammer of every thought of the abuses and blaming her for the headache when it was I who was wielding the hammer all those years. Silly human! I mean, I was plain stupid really.

It would be several years later, until I would be able to achieve a fully engaged, relationship with my mother based on pure divine love and gratitude and appreciation for her. I had to integrate my forgiveness and find out who I was if I didn't blame her anymore and, to be honest, I still hadn't discovered radical responsibility which would come years later. It has taken me time to rise into the fullness and truth of who I really am—the

Universe wrapped in stardust—and to see that there is only love so there is never anything to forgive because I (the Universe) do not make mistakes and all is always perfect.

Most of us wake up slowly, thank GOD. (*You're welcome.*) If we were to just pop awake it would blow our circuits and we might find ourselves unable to function in our families and society. Therefore we awaken as the caterpillar transforms . . . perfectly and according to the divine plan that knows just where and when the conductor of the symphony of all creation is going to call on us to sing and play and heal and forgive and expand.

RADICAL HONESTY

Radical honesty is telling the objective truth. It is the truth that exists behind our beliefs and our stories and our programs, and the meaning we've constructed around our experiences. It is the truth we do not speak because we fear the external world's response to it. We fear anger, hurt, loss of approval or friendship, or needing to expend energy on the argument we are sure will ensue. Instead we are nice or polite, or we make commitments we later regret. Radical honesty is the truth that sets us and others free.

This is a precious and powerful gift when given benevolently and with permission. But it can cause great pain and inflict deep wounds when given irresponsibly, selfishly, and without permission, or when the other is not ready for it.

There are three levels of honesty that I will speak to here. Each has a varying degree of impact, depth, potency, and intimacy. Radical honesty, like everything else in every moment, is a choice. As stated above, it carries with it great responsibility and it must be respected and used with care and permission. But underneath everything, honesty is honesty, period.

Casual honesty. Casual honesty is the quality and degree of honesty we bring to casual conversations with friends, acquaintances, loved ones, coworkers, and strangers. We all know this level of honesty, although we may not have explored it or sought to understand it as separate from some of the deeper or more potent levels of honesty. We are operating at the level of casual honesty when someone asks us how we are doing today and we respond, "I'm fine" or "good." We usually answer this way because we don't desire to share more or go into the details.

Now don't confuse this with casual *dishonesty*, like when someone asks, "How does this dress look?" and we say, "Fine," when what we really believe is, "It's hideous, burn that ugly thing!" Honesty is still honesty and dishonesty is still dishonesty. Get it?

So when I say, "I'm fine," in response to, "How are you?" it truly represents my state of being albeit in the most diluted and general sense if I'm being radically honest. We are not required to give detail to be honest. Others may want, or even think they need, more details and some people might not be satisfied by our general, diluted response to their question and so may start to poke and prod and inquire for more detail.

Honesty cloaked in vagueness is still honesty. Without story or explanation or detail, it is just diluted or general. We are the ones who get to choose the level of detail we want to include when we're being honest, based on the situation, our relationship to the receiver of the information we're offering, the depths we are prepared to delve into, and the impact we desire to have.

We may decide to succumb to the next level of inquiry if we CHOOSE to. But if we succumb to questioning when we do not want to, then we are not being honest with ourselves and we often regret it afterward. Regret is a very good sign that we've not been honest with ourselves or others. It is a sign that what we wanted was dishonored in favor of what another person wanted from us or for us! Although sometimes we can be convinced to "go to the concert" and find that we have had a fantastic time and are glad we succumbed, that is an exception, not the rule. Regret generally helps us learn and be better discerners in the future.

What is important is that we examine and are aware of when we feel regret. For instance, realizing that we said yes when we meant no and then owning it.

The point of casual honesty as a category is that we can choose the potency of the truth we wish to convey based on a myriad of circumstances. This is our right. For example, someone might ask us, "Where were you last night?" To which we might respond: "I went to dinner with a friend." We keep the response casually honest because we don't actually want to say, "I was out to dinner with Ryan, who I know you hate, because then I'm going to have to deal with all your drama and emotions and judgment about my choice to go to dinner with Ryan, which depending on your mood is a process that could last an hour, a day, or a month." We CHOOSE a less potent truth because we want to keep moving forward and do not want to disrupt the moment and create a separate event out of answering a question.

Here's another simple example of this. Let's say we have plans to head out with friends for a fun night and we are moving things along, but there is, among the group, a friend who just takes forever, always. This friend typically changes multiple times, redoes her hair, and yet always looks the same to us. And what does our friend ask repeatedly? "How do I look?"

And what do we repeatedly say? "Great! Let's go!" (We dare not say, "Fine," or else we'll get the speech about the word *fine*— you know the one.) The point is, we just want to get to the fun. We don't want to create an "event" with this person about preparing to have fun that could literally suck up an hour and result is us talking, again, about how our friend's mother was always critical of her and that's why she obsesses about how he looks. It just is what it is. It's the friend's one quirk and we are friends so we should deal with it. We avoid all that by saying, "Great!" because, in fact, our friend always does look great and we don't want to deal.

Now we could choose to bring radical honesty to all our casual encounters if we wanted to, but then we'd be one of those annoying people who think it is their job to tell everyone their truth about everything and follow it up with, "Hey, I'm just being honest!"

No, you're just being annoying and no one wants to hang out with you.

Ever wonder why you have to work so hard to find out what's going on, on a Friday? Exactly . . .

This is not the type of radical honesty we are talking about. Just wanted to make that 100 percent clear.

Disruptive honesty. Disruptive honesty creates an event. It pulls focus from whatever happens to be going on and requires everyone present to deal with a "truth": to work it out, to listen, to learn, to grow.

I'm NOT talking about the people that create an issue out of everything so that they can constantly argue and debate about it. That's *drama!* There's a big, big difference. I'm talking about honesty driven by a desire to improve or evolve a situation or relationship.

Context is important here. Timing is important here. The depth of the relationship you have with the recipient is important here. You need to be CONSCIOUS about all of these factors before you run around and start throwing disruptive honesty up all over everyone and you eventually become their least favorite person. Because, let's face it, honest vomit is still vomit. It's messy and no one likes it. (Been there, done that—so my advice is don't. Just don't).

The other piece that is required here besides being conscious is getting permission. Especially in the beginning, when you start to use this level of radical honesty. It's what saves you from becoming the vomiting honesty guy. You ask permission before you share. And if you get a no, you STOP. You don't keep asking until you get a yes or keep posing the question differently until you get a yes. One no and you stop. No means no! Period. No buts.

Now, when you get good at listening to the Universe, and I mean really good, you will know when she is demanding that you be honest because this moment is the ripest, most opportune moment to deliver this particular truth because another's soul actually wants it and their human side is also ready for the resulting shift. Then you don't need to ask permission. But don't please don't try this right away. Practice for a while first. It took me YEARS and lots of big, ugly, vomity messes before I learned this. If you are just starting out, you MUST get permission. Always. I still require myself to get permission to this day.

Regardless my strong insistence here, I know many of you

will get self-righteous with the truth as I did and you will serve it up sloppy. That's fine. Go ahead. You too will learn by trial and error until you refine your approach and master the effective use of this powerful tool of disruptive honesty.

So let's return to the example above in which someone has asked, "Where were you last night?" This time, let's change the circumstances a bit. The person asking is now a good friend who we love and adore and who we also think is being an idiot about the whole Ryan thing. Furthermore, we are over having to walk on egg shells so our friend doesn't get upset. In this instance, we might ask: "Do you want the whole truth or just the general truth?"

This is asking permission.

I'm going to assume the friend choses the former, the whole truth, for the sake of this example. Hearing this, we say: "I was at dinner with Ryan." Now if or when our friend starts in with all the BS and drama and emotion and stories about Ryan that we suspected would come and which is why we pondered answering the question more generally, we take the opportunity created by this disruption to say lovingly to our friend, "STOP!"

Our friend will probably continue with his Ryan diatribe, which we will now disrupt with whatever physical or audible cues we need to employ. I sometimes like the using the hand in the face with the phrase "STOP," being repeated again. But be careful, this can also really set some people off. Be discerning. Feel into and know before you act.

By *physical cues,* I don't mean a slap or punch. Do not touch your friend. Use gestures. Flail your arms or whatever. Once the friend finally stops talking you can proceed into the moment you have disrupted and begin to work with him to create a different future together.

At this juncture, you might say, "I love you and I'm tired of dealing with your issues with Ryan. That shit happened three months ago (or whatever the time frame). Let it go. He is my friend and he is going to continue to be my friend, and I am going continue to see him. And you need to either deal with that, because I'm done arguing about it and hearing about it, or we can stop seeing each other until you can deal with it. Either way I'm done. I'm not going to have this kind of interaction with you again."

From this point, the scene can go in many directions, depending on how attached your friend is to his story and how committed he is to being victimized by Ryan even though Ryan has been out of the picture for however long. What's important to realize here is that you are taking care of yourself (see the next Radical, *radical self-care*) AND you are taking care of your friend because he is allowing the Ryan event to continue to poison his life and your friendship, and you are saying ENOUGH. You are not demanding your friend change or be different. You have to be fine with whatever he chooses. But you can outline what the consequences of the choice will be.

If your friend chooses to continue to poison his present and future, and your friendship with him with the Ryan event, radical responsibility allows that you to choose no longer to spend time with him. Not as a punishment. But rather because it serves your peace of mind to do so and allows you to create the reality you want to experience. It is your friend's choice first. And then it is yours second.

The opportunity in a disrupted moment like this one is HUGE! For both of you! Equally! When we do this right, radical honesty is a gift that gives to all.

Now I'll give you an example of a moment I did not want to disrupt with radical honesty. Well, at first I didn't, but then the Universe insisted I do so after the fact and I did. The result was so spectacularly beautiful it brought me and my good friend to tears and the impact was life changing!

I had noticed that this particular friend, who was so extraordinary in almost every way, would sometimes resort to deceit and manipulation to get what he wanted. I also noticed that he was unaware that he was doing this. I also knew enough about him to realize that it was a program that was created back in his childhood that was so deep, he did it without even consciously thinking about it. And usually this program was employed when he wanted to avoid the unpleasantness that the truth would bring or wanted a particular outcome, but instead of just stating his desire to a group and allowing a discussion to occur and then going with the will of the group, he would have quiet side conversations that planted seeds of his new plan in people's minds or he would tell one person that another didn't really want to follow the original plan, so "maybe we should consider a new plan." Of course, this was not true, but it was part of the program.

I watched this happen once. I saw it all. I knew exactly when the program started. I saw it in action and then, "TAH DAH" I saw the plan change as if by magic and really without the full consensus of the group. When this happened, I declared that I wanted to stick with the original plan and my declaration gave others who weren't as willing as me to speak up and express their own wants. Once people felt they had permission to say, "Me too," the group went in two separate directions.

I'll point out that the machinations and manipulations in this scenario had started the night before and lasted until morning. So much time and energy were being spent for the machination and the drama which could have easily been avoided. After it all played out I made my good friend aware that I had seen it all: the lies, the manipulation, the deceit, the machinations. I told him when it had started and how he had done it and I told him that it was not OK with me. Also I told him that this was beneath him and not necessary because our group was capable of changing plans or addressing his wants directly. I told him NEVER to do this again to me or in my presence and I gave him permission to be radically honest with me the next time and promised I would honor his honesty.

For me, the key factor in being disruptively honest with my friend was that this man was part of my inner circle of most trusted friends. He was like a brother. Had it been someone else in the group whom I did not know as well I would simply have gathered whoever else wanted to stick with the original plan and been done with it. But this was one of my best friends who was lying to and manipulating me when he didn't even have to. And truly it wasn't even him doing it, it was an old program that he learned years earlier in order to get what he wanted and needed.

Fast forward six-plus months. It happened again. And again

I watched the whole thing unfolding. Around the same time, my friend also responded to some business inquiries I made with mistruths that later revealed themselves. (Coincidence? The Universe says, "OH NO"). On this occasion, I thought about whether or not I wanted to orchestrate a disruptively honest experience over all this and I ultimately decided to let it ALL go: the three separate events, two of lying and one of manipulation. I moved on.

Then suddenly, one day, maybe two weeks later, the Universe said, "You will not let this go. It is important that you give this friend the gift of honesty NOW! And it is important that you hit him hard with it, because he is ready to get it. The opportunity is ripe for a breakthrough." And I listened because she spoke so clearly and directly. And I hit him with it HARD.

We have to understand that sometimes it takes force to dislodge an old program that does not want to die. It takes a powerful disruptive event to break it loose and bring it into conscious awareness to be released.

It is important to note that when I spoke to my friend to deliver my radical honesty, I did not make him bad or wrong. I came from "I" and told him how I felt and what my choices were in response to his choices. I told him that my inner circle is a sanctuary where I can let down my guard and be without judgment or worry of betrayal or dishonesty. Very few people occupy this place in my life. It is an honored and special place, it is my safe place that I populate it only with individuals that Spirit has chosen to bring and weave tightly together. I said his behavior was unacceptable to me and that I would not tolerate it. I even reminded him that I previously warned him not to engage in such dishonesty and had empowered him with permission to speak truthfully to me, to practice radical honesty.

Finally, I said that if my friendship was the price he must pay to learn this lesson and break this pattern then so be it. And I left it at that.

My friend responded with denial and then anger. But I stood in my truth because I knew that this is what programs and the mind do, and how they respond when they are threatened and seen. Their survival depends on it. These are the death throes of a program recognized. At this time I was also able to pull slightly away from my friend, physically leaving on a weeklong business trip, after the confrontation. The distance both gave him time to process what I said and experience what the loss of friendship would feel like. And it gave him the opportunity to choose the friendship OR choose the program, knowing he could not keep both.

When I returned home, my friend asked to see me. I could feel that he had surrendered and had allowed the loving act of telling him the truth to penetrate to the deepest level of his being and to separate truth from program. He came to me in tears. Messy, heaving tears. I had never before seen him cry like this. He sat on my couch and cried and cried and cried before he could get to a place where he could speak. And I cried at the beauty of it. The perfection of it. "Thank you, Spirit," I said. "You are so beautiful and wise. Thank you for pushing me to share the gift of radical honesty with my friend."

When my friend composed himself and spoke, he said, "Thank you, brother! I see now the courage and love it took for you to be as brutally honest with me as you were. I see and know the gift of it. I have examined the cause of this program and traced it to its root! The behavior you pointed out to me was a behavior I learned to get what I wanted from my mom and dad because it was the only way I could. But I see now that our friendship, and life in general, does not require this behavior, and that all I need do to get what I want is ask for it or choose it. I've overcomplicated things for so long, running around working extra hard to make sure the end result is what I want, that I forgot or just didn't see that I could be direct and simply ask. I am not that boy anymore. I am a man and I can and I will do it differently."

After he said this, we both cried together and our friendship grew deeper and stronger. The moment showed me how each of us holds tools and gifts for others, which can help others to awaken and learn and remember. In this case, it was the gift of honesty. The moment also proved that there is a loving Universe conspiring with us and drawing us toward each other so that we can awaken and remember together!

This is the power of radical honesty at its best.

Myth-busting honesty. Myth-busting honesty leads us to the absolutely objective, unvarnished, nonfiction truths that exist beneath our stories, programs, and beliefs that, when discovered or remembered and fully integrated with what we already know and feel, shatter our illusions and reconcile false realities. Typically the mind constructs false realities to make sense of painful events and circumstances that are beyond our ability to comprehend when they happen. If we do not have all the information, it is a human tendency to fill in the blanks with false data and guesses. For instance, how my child mind wrapped my early abuse in the veil of a dream of a monster at the door of our house.

A myth is a memory of "reality" that in no way resembles the truth. For instance, some choose the belief that a perfect newborn baby is born into sin and if the baby dies without being absolved of it by a human, the baby will burn for eternity in the fires of hell—even if the baby lives only for a few hours after birth. This is a powerful myth in my opinion!

Regardless of where myths or beliefs come from—whether internally created or externally forced upon us at an impressionable time in our development—one thing is true, any myth that does not equal truth imprisons us and hinders our discovery of our own truth or a truth beyond the myth into which we were born and indoctrinated. There are too many examples of this to name, but let's just bring our attention to some that we now consider silly ones. Like the myth that the sun revolved around the Earth. This was a powerful myth in its time in Europe. Rather than accept any truth other than this one, or any proof of a truth other than this one, people were actually killed to defend it. Yes, KILLED! To defend a false truth, an indoctrinated belief. To defend a myth. This is how powerful stories and myths can be and how scary it can be to even consider that certain myths that define our reality might not be true. It's so scary sometimes that we'd rather continue to believe false truths than to expand our thinking and knowing to include a new truth. Powerful, powerful stuff.

Humanity has fought wars and millions have died to defend our myths, our constructs of the mind to explain unexplainable realities that gain broader agreement until they are widely accepted as truth. *Bingo, bango, bongo.* Belief created.

Now let's go with something much smaller and simpler, maybe a personal belief like "Dogs are scary monsters that can destroy us." If you walk down a street in any city and polled one hundred people, they would, in varying degrees, either disagree or agree with this belief. The people who believe it utterly often have severe anxiety around dogs; they might even start shaking or crying if a dog gets near them. The people who completely disagree probably are dog lovers and have lived with dogs their whole lives and see these creatures as family or their best friends. The objective truth about dogs is that they are domesticated animals that can be loving and kind on one end of the spectrum or ferocious and dangerous on the other, and we should exercise keen observation and proper caution to ascertain the truth of a given dog and its training and then respond accordingly.

Myth-busting honesty is honesty that when spoken, shared, communicated, or discovered has the power to shatter our beliefs, stories, and myths, and free us to create new futures that would have otherwise not occurred.

I'll go back to the example I gave above where the Universe told me to hit my friend hard with a disruptive truth about his manipulation and deceit because his behavior was intolerable to me. In this case, the disruptive truth helped him end a program and made room for new possibilities in our friendship. But when I described my observations and my point of view about them, I was also telling him a myth-busting truth that freed my friend from an unconscious program that made him choose deceit and manipulation to get what we wanted. Then he replaced the myth with the truth that he could simply ask for what he wanted directly! Simple. Powerful. True. And just like that, he was free. At least from that myth.

Remember, radical honesty is both a magical wand and a weapon. It can both heal and wound. If you use it to wound, then you are creating suffering and suffering will be the price you pay. If you use it to heal and help people to remember their authentic selves and elevate their circumstances the result will be the gift of improving your life. Radical honesty is beautiful because it has so many facets. When I meet people who are living as THEMSELVES, unapologetically authentically, I know it right away and I am drawn to them because they are radical honesty personified.

By contrast, when I meet people who are chameleons, always changing who they are to fit in and accommodate and please, like I used to, I want to run far from them fast because they do not know themselves at all. They only know themselves in what others want them to be or do or say. I love them anyway, and I know they will learn or they won't, and regardless of whether or not they do learn, they are loved by a Universe that can do nothing but love them. Still, I prefer the company of authentic people.

I could write a whole book on the power of radical honesty and how to use it benevolently, but I think this material will suffice for now. Play with this new form of honesty. Use it kindly. Be gentle with yourself and others. Start small. Exercise the atrophied radical honesty muscle in you before you try the equivalent of lifting a horse or swimming the English Channel. Too much radical honesty too soon and you may hurt yourself or others, and I don't want that for you. I know you don't want that for yourself either.

RADICAL SELF-CARE

Radical self-care makes itself known in the power of NO and in the power of YES, both uttered with increasing clarity, confidence, consciousness, and intention. It is the tool that ultimately breaks every pattern of dysfunction and codependence in our relationships. For when we truly take care of ourselves, we allow no one to abuse us, take advantage of us, or trespass against us.

Through radical self-care we learn that when we do not fight for ourselves, love ourselves, respect ourselves, and deliberately care for ourselves we suffer, because we compromise and give away pieces of ourselves until there is nothing left to give. We eventually become depleted and resentful and full of regret. And our relationships and our families and our jobs and our communities and our nations and our planet suffers the loss of the unique and brilliant gift the Universe intended us to be.

So take care of you! You deserve it. You've earned it. It is your right. Do it now. Right now. Stop, take a breath, and do something that takes care of YOU even if that something is small. Do it. Just make sure that it truly honors you on the deepest level. Honors the YOU you've been searching for and desire to come home to. No matter your circumstances, no matter the life you see when you look around you, you can break the cycle and stop giving pieces of yourself away to others.

You don't have to give pieces of yourself away to your friends because they pressure you to or because they want to keep you small. You don't have to give pieces of yourself away to your parents because they express displeasure at some of your life choices or want something different for YOUR life. You don't have to give pieces of yourself away to your kids or to your spouse who you struggle to love because you both are changing and life is just so busy that you don't know how else to stay together other than to pretend nothing has changed. I am taking this to the extreme of course. Exaggerating for effect. But it is not far from true for many. I have met you and I have listened, and I have watched you on reality TV. These are real issues. *Mmm hmm.*

Even if only a few of the scenarios I've just described pertain to you, it means you are still giving away pieces of yourself in order to please or appease or get approval from, or be liked, by someone else—and let's be candid, you only have so many pieces to give until you start to feel the loss of YOU. This is problematic. We've all seen what happens when we run out of pieces to give, it gets messy! It sure got messy for me at nineteen. My ME bag was empty. But that's what it took for me to start the journey back to me. But don't wait until you are so fed up and drained by giving yourself away that you have to go to such DRASTIC measures to bring yourself back into balance.

We've all heard stories of these folks, dads or moms who just walk out one day never to return. They had wandered too far from their paths and had nothing left to give, so in order to survive they just up and walked away. We all know people on the edge of this, because all they do is complain about EVERYTHING—their jobs, their bodies, their spouses, their kids—as if all these things just happened to them suddenly and without warning. We also see younger people who have only been giving themselves away for a short while, but you can hear them starting to give up on their dreams because they've got responsibilities now, such as a spouse, a job, kids, and a house.

Wherever you find yourself on the continuum of giving yourself away, there you are. You've done your best. You are here and this is where you can start to do it differently. This is where you can start to reclaim the pieces you've given away and put Humpty Dumpty back together again.

My own breakdown came early. I don't know if this is good or bad—well, I actually know that it's neither good nor bad, but some might say I'm lucky and some might say "Damn, you are still all kinds of messy, even after thirty years of collecting those pieces and putting them back together!" And probably both would be true simultaneously. Like mastering all the Radicals: It took me a long time to learn the "how to" and far too long to put a name to what I was doing so that I could do it more consciously.

Trust me, wherever you are, however difficult your situation, you can start now. And you will thank yourself for it. Your family and friends will thank you for it. Your community will thank you for it and the Universe herself will cry and cheer and look all a mess with her mascara running because she is so glad you have done it!

Any cycle of giving in or giving away can be broken when we learn radical self-care. If we take the first step we will be rewarded for our courage. I promise. Like with any of the other Radicals. Start small. Do something different. Say yes when you mean yes (or no when you mean no) to take care of yourself. Practice this principle with someone safe. We all have that someone in our lives. Talk to your safe person about it and let this individual know you need support. You want to learn how to say no when you mean no and yes ONLY when you mean yes. You want to learn to live for you! And to make time for what you want and need.

I won't lie and say that it is going to be easy, because people in your life are going to expect you to continue to be the person you've been. When you start practicing radical self-care they will up their game to turn your nos into yeses or vice versa. They like your yeses better because it means you pretend to agree even when you don't, that you'll join them when you don't want to, or that you'll do it even though you don't want to—and that serves them, not you. They are not bad or wrong for wanting this. You have trained them to be this way by repeating your accommodating behavior over and over. Many will say, "Honey, what's wrong with you?" or "Is something wrong?" or "Are you all right?" To which you can and should answer, "I'm getting there!"

If you don't want to make dinner, don't make dinner. That's why we invented take out. If you don't want to clean up yet another of your family's or roommate's messes, don't—make your spouse or your children or your roommate contribute where appropriate. And oh my, they will complain and whine and protest. And if that happens, complain and whine and protest every time they ask you to do something for them until they see how silly it sounds. You trained them, and you can untrain them. You aren't doing them any favors allowing them to just take take take from you.

Trust me. If you don't want to have sex with your partner on "sex night," don't. If you don't want to go to lunch with your mother so she can complain about your father or her friend or criticize your significant other, don't, and tell her the honest reason why you're not going so she has an opportunity to do and be better.

Radical self-care requires all the radicals. That's why I put it last. Some of you might master this one first. Good for you. Not me. This one was hard for me because I wanted to fit in and be liked, and so I did and said many things that I didn't want to do to achieve this. Radical self-care requires courage. It requires honesty. It requires you to forgive yourself for the mess you created before you can even take step one toward doing it differently. It requires responsibility, because you wouldn't even attempt it unless you had some grasp of the fact that you got yourself here and can take yourself elsewhere.

I've said it before and I'll say it again: Now is a new moment in your life. A blank canvas. A clean slate. Pause and wake up right now. Prove this to yourself by showing yourself that you are free to stand or sit. Walk or run. Move left or right. Sing or scream. And if you have these options then don't you also have the bigger options? You can start making bigger choices that take care of you because otherwise you will sleep-create more of what you don't want and CTRL C + CTRL V yesterday into tomorrow. Ten years from now you'll wake up and nothing will have changed except that you will have less of you for all the pieces of yourself you gave away in those ten years and then you'll have to do more work to gather them all up. And if this is what you choose, another ten years of the same, the Universe will celebrate and love you for it. But is that what you really want?

So gather your courage. Start small and practice and get strong. Find others trying to do the same. Get help. But do something different so that you can experience something different and make some progress on the road back to YOU.

CHAPTER ELEVEN

MY IMPACT BEYOND ME

*If you are at war with yourself or with anything
or anyone you perceive as separate from you,
then silly, silly human, you slumber still.*

Every day we either contribute to the malady of thought that inflicts humanity or we contribute to the healing of it. Period. We're either part of the problem or part of the solution. When we truly awaken we understand that everything is perfect, exactly as it is because it is and if we desire to create something better, we can by simply choosing it.

When we come home to ourselves and who we are, there can be only peace within and among and between. If there is not, if we still struggle and "war against," then we are not yet HOME. Even though we struggle against what is so vehemently and righteously and beautifully, through truly awakened eyes we can see that the infinite Universe in its infinite wisdom and infinite power to create and destroy accepts and adores the perfection of everything everywhere just as it is in this very moment, for if it wanted it to be different than it is, it already would be.

The Universe celebrates our struggle against. She dances to it as she would to the sound of the most beautiful music because the dance helps her know this aspect of herself better. By knowing and mastering struggle, she can know, and then master, ease—through us.

Struggle between two opposites or between opposing beliefs is a human invention. Where else in creation do we see this but in the realm of humans? Animals and plants may compete for resources or for the territory in which those resources exist, or may fight for access to a womb in which to plant their seeds, but theirs is not the struggle of disagreement. It is not a struggle born of a desire to be right. Nor is it to defend a myth or story, as we humans do because our fear of living outside our myth or story is too great. The struggles and battles we see in nature are those of evolution in action, of creation becoming better—more complex, refined, and exquisite.

So why do humans engage in struggle? Why do we war against, well, everything? We do so for only one reason, FEAR! We fear that without our constructs, our stories, our myths, our beliefs, our laws, our judgments, our separation we would drown in the infinite sea that is the totality of creation. This terrifies us so much that we would rather kill or torture or hate or destroy those parts of ourselves (other humans) that we now perceive as separate because we have forgotten who we are. They are the parts of us that we would know as our brothers and sisters if we only saw them for who they truly are: fellow drops within a vast ocean experiencing a brief adventure in singularity.

While we sleep in forgetfulness we war against our parents, authority, Christians, Jews, Muslims, people with a different skin color than ours, geniuses, idiots, the awakened, and the unawakened. We also war within an illusion of wakefulness. We war against the system, racism, poverty, war, governments, corporations, institutions, pollution, communism, and capitalism. If you are at war with yourself or with anything or anyone you perceive as separate from you, then silly, silly human, you slumber still and awakened you are NOT. The energy of struggle is struggle no matter what struggles against what or who struggles against whom, or for what reason. The energy of war is war. The energy of judgment is judgment. The energy of hate is hate. Just as the energy of love is love and the energy of joy is joy and the energy of fun is fun. It is all energy, our thoughts, our emotions, our words, and our actions.

So when I talk about our impact beyond us, what I'm talking about is the frequency of the energy you are sending forth from your body and mind to your family, friends, workplace, community, state, country, and planet. What is the contribution you are making? If you think you don't matter, think again. If you think a thought doesn't matter or a word or an action, think again! They matter! Ponder for a moment the power of a single thought (or word or action) in history. We must come to know and be responsible for and master our energetic output, the frequency we contribute to all that is. This is the note we sing, the light we shine.

The Universe cares about the energy of your thoughts or words or actions, the frequency of them. She cares about the quality of the energy you choose to "feel" in response to your thoughts and stories. So stop now and survey your day, at whatever point you awaken in it, and review the quality of your thoughts and words, actions and interactions, and be radically honest with yourself. What is the quality of the energy that you are broadcasting into the Universe today? Is it kindness or cruelty? Is it love or fear? Is it ease or struggle? Is it war against an idea, a group, an institution, a culture, a religion? Is it joy and love because you know that (Y)OUR creation is exactly as it should be right now simply because it is and because it could be no other way than this or it would be?

The single most powerful thing we can do as individual fragments of totality experiencing momentary separation from itself is to consciously choose the quality of the energy we emanate into the field of humanity, the Earth, and the whole of the Universe.

Look to Mahatma Gandhi and Nelson Mandela for examples of this. They experienced great injustices and suffering, but instead of choosing to respond as others have responded to similar situations with hatred and anger and war against they chose a way of peace—both inner and outer. Mandela chose to be free inside his prison. Gandhi knew that to war against the great British Empire was futile, so he stood in the truth of what he believed and he lived that truth and that truth shone in him, through him, and all around him. By doing so, he moved mountains and made changes that the world thought impossible. The point is that they chose who and what and how they would be. They chose love and light and the expression of their radiance and truth, and the choice was powerful, so powerful, in fact, that it emancipated whole peoples from political and cultural enslavement. Had they chosen as most others chose—to war against—they would have lost and we would not know them as the heroes they are today.

We always have a choice in response to any word or action or situation, even when we do not feel or see the choice. If we could slow down time, we would see that there is a moment, even if only a small one, during which we chose our response. So take radical responsibility for your choices, and when you can, when you are awakened to them in the moment, choose the quality of the energy you express into the universe. As the saying goes, "Be the change you want to see in the world." It all starts with YOU.

Don't wait until the situation or another person changes, be radically courageous and go first. Demonstrate what it looks like for the Universe to live and express through you, and choose love and kindness. Do not be small or petty or righteous. YOU ARE GOD. Own it! Own what that means. For if you continue to choose anger and hate and judgment and war and struggle against, then I assure you, you slumber still. You are NOT awakened. PERIOD.

But that's OK. We all slumber occasionally. I myself slumber often. Sometimes they are long naps and I drool terribly and fart in my sleep. GROSS. But as I continue to commit myself to being part of the metamorphosis of humanity and I am able to see the harm that sleep-creating inflicts upon my relationships, humanity, and the planet, I will work harder to wake my ass up, clean it up (the mess), take responsibility for it, and DO BETTER in the next moment. Because I can.

There is a particular example in today's popular culture that stands out as a daily reminder to all of us to do better and be better. It is at the end of every episode of The Ellen DeGeneres Show when Ellen says, "Be kind to one another." This idea makes me smile. It lifts me up. And it is as if the Universe herself is reminding me to be kinder and I do because of this reminder. We all need reminders every day to do and be better, to be kinder, more YOU than in the previous moment or the previous day. And most importantly, be kind to yourself! Forgive yourself immediately and completely when you discover that you have fallen asleep at the wheel of your creation bus and are doing some serious "Dang, I'm gonna need to fix that" damage! Wake up, laugh, and then love the perfection of even the ugliness that you created during your slumber. Look to the back of the bus and see the bratty child, the ferocious beast, and each of the seven dwarves that live inside you and put a song on the sound system and sing and dance with them. Thank them for helping create the experience that helps you wake up and do you better.

Remember that every little bit counts. Even if you only do one act of kindness or achieve one true expression of your gifts and divinity in a day or week, this is monumental and it means you deserve cake with candles and presents! Perhaps tomorrow you will be able to express yourself twice and be kind three times, until suddenly you see that your energy has shifted and the quality of energy you are broadcasting into the field of creation is more aligned with who you truly are. Perhaps then you will be able to perceive the ballet of souls dancing around you every day. Doing their best. Struggling, achieving, falling, and rising, and desiring to come home to themselves, too.

We think we are powerless in a world that seems dominated by money and fear and commerce and a struggle for power. We are not. We are powerful beyond measure, always and in all ways. Nelson Mandela found freedom in a jail cell—pure, unbridled freedom. If one of us can find freedom within his prison, then all of us are capable of it. During his lifetime, Mandela wrote and spoke about how when he was set free from that South African prison, he knew that if he left with hatred in his heart for those who had imprisoned him then he would be carrying his prison with him, and so he forgave them. And so can we. If you perceive that you are imprisoned by a system, a relationship, a religion, a culture, a government, or a race of sentient reptilians from another planet, know it is you who are imprisoning yourself. I have met people who have everything in the world they could ever want—money, power, material possessions—yet they are imprisoned by their beliefs, stories, and perceived limitations.

And I have met people who have absolutely nothing who sing, dance, and celebrate. And I've met many people on the spectrum between these extremes.

If you want to change your government, vote. If you want to disempower a corporation, then spend your money elsewhere. You do have power, you do matter, and you can make a difference all by yourself, just by being authentically YOU and choosing what comes next in the freedom of the next moment. You don't need to push, cajole, scream, or demand that anyone else wake up and agree with you for change to happen. You can show, by example, what it looks like to come home to YOU. Show what it looks like to be kind and to forgive, take responsibility, be honest, and have courage. You can make no greater contribution than this. Take care of yourself, let others take care of themselves, and let the Universe direct us all—the actors, musicians, and dancers—in this wondrous rom-com horror-drama called life.

CHAPTER TWELVE

TAME THE BEAST

To reinstall the operating system
of the Creator HERSELF,
you need only go to one place: NATURE,
the ultimate app store.

have done much exploring and adventuring into the realms of my mind. The two of us (my mind and I) have a love/hate relationship, but I must admit that it is getting better every day. I am not a psychologist or neuropsychologist. Nor am I an expert on brain anatomy or chemistry. Neuroscience and chemistry are vast and complicated fields of study. But do you know what? I am an expert on MY OWN MIND. I have been the victim of its abuses, taunting, and fears, and I have benefitted from its brilliance and ability to learn and make sense of my experiences. In my personal studies and interactions with my mind, I have come to believe that the human mind is basically programmed through experiences to achieve system conformity and avoid pain.

Unfortunately, the same systems that program the mind—our families, societies, cultures, and religions—often teach us that our souls' deepest desires and purposes are impractical, irresponsible, impossible, or inappropriate. Armed with this programming, our minds run our lives and find ways to keep delivering the same internalized messages to us over and over and over and over again. But it is not the fault of our minds, as they are just doing as they were told, as they were programmed.

Humanity is collectively suffering from malady of the mind and we can only heal this malady by bringing the mind back into balance with the rest of our instrument: mind, body, and soul.

Love your mind. It is a most wondrous creation! Complex and beautiful, it only desires to do as instructed and achieve the goals set out for it, including the goal of keeping us safe. Most of us eventually wake up to the fact that conformity, safety, and pain avoidance do not equal happiness, fulfillment, or even mild satisfaction. We discover that they, in fact, lead to frustration, depression, anxiety, and sadness, the pain of which fuels our search and awakening. It's a beautiful dance really, but when you're in it, it is anything but pleasant.

I feel for the mind. At times I am even sad for it. It just tries and tries and learns and learns, so that we can navigate this reality with as little pain as possible and without looking like idiots in the process. But we are idiots. We are complex beings born into a complex reality, and most of the time we have no idea what we are doing. There is no manual. No HELP link. No 1-800 number to call when we can't figure out how to navigate a situation or relationship without totally messing that shit up. So we do our best and our mind does its best. By design, we both forgot that there is a force around and within us that seeks to gently guide us home and toward the fullest expression of OURSELVES. We have collectively forgotten this because we do not perceive the force I'm referring to with our five senses or through our minds alone—though to be fair, the mind has some capacity to open and perceive the force.

The Universe herself is the force at work actualizing the potential of everything. Look to nature if you question this truth.

Humans are the ONLY animals on this planet that struggle to be who and what we are. We struggle to know our place and purpose because we get trapped by a mind that's been programmed by an unnatural, humanmade system. Yet we must also realize that these humanmade systems exist within the natural system and so we can, at any time, shift our focus and attention and presence to the system that gave birth to us, the system that was designed to govern this world and is ultimately governing this world.

A perfect system created all that is on this planet: every grain of sand and every bird, mammal, tree, blade of grass, insect, and fish, and yes, every human being, on this planet. Although we may have ceased to trust this miracle maker, preferring instead to trust the mechanics of our limited minds, which cannot fully comprehend the enormity of the miracle we live inside of every day, the fact that we breathe air, our hearts beat, and trillions of electric and chemical impulses happen inside us in every minute are proof of an intelligent presence in and around us. This moment and every moment is a miracle guided and architected by a benevolent, loving, intelligent, living Universe that only wants one thing: to know itself through us and the rest of its creations, to experience through our eyes, ears, skin, noses, tongues, and minds.

It is time to embrace the mind, thank it for its service, forgive it for the suffering it has caused us (or if we are to be radically honest, the suffering we have allowed it to cause us), and relieve it of its burdensome responsibilities so that it can rest, heal, and ultimately come into balance with the other parts of us. It is time for each of us to wipe our minds clean of the fears and patterns and programs and beliefs of a disconnected human-made systems based on myths, fears, shoulds, conformity, and wounds from painful experiences. It is time to defrag our hard drives, reboot, and then reinstall the operating system that lives within all things, conducts the symphony of all life, and pushes all creatures forward into their own possibilities and becomingness.

This operating system is not new, so let's stop calling for a *new* operating system to heal humanity and Earth. This operating system is all around us and within us already, working its magic and creating miracles every second of every day. We have attacked it with viruses of thought, written programs over it, and fought against it, yet it remains constant and present and benevolent. Right now, it waits within and around you for you to stop doing and trying and struggling and thinking so that it and you can dance together and rise.

To reinstall this operating system, you need only go to one place: NATURE, the ultimate app store. While there, feel the connection, see how things dance with each other, and observe the interplay between different species and forces within concentric shared ecosystems. Open your heart and quiet your mind, and the reinstall program will begin, below thought. Once the force that is all around you reboots and reawakens within you, a new phase of your life can begin.

The operating system of nature is not based on analysis or rational thought; it is based on trust, inner knowing, connectedness, and the endless possibilities of the Universe. This is the operating system of the Creator HERSELF. It has always been within you, waiting to be reactivated, and it is at work even now. You were born with it, as all of us were born with it. It is part of our DNA and our connection to the Earth, the galaxy, and beyond. You cannot *not* have it. The mere fact that we exist demonstrates that this Universal operating system is within us. How else could a mother's body construct a new vehicle for an adventurous soul? How else could a flower bloom or an egg give rise to a baby chicken born knowing what to eat, fear, and do to survive? This operating system connects All That Is to All That Is. It is the fabric of creation. Separation from it is an illusion.

It is impossible to live within creation and be separate from it. Yet we have learned to identify with our separateness instead of our connectedness, which is akin to identifying with an illusion or fictitious reality. It is like watching a movie and believing you are a character within it and then staying in character after the film ends. Silly, silly humans.

I liken the mind to an undisciplined child. We've all seen them in the store or at a restaurant. When they aren't getting their ways or they are frightened or overstimulated, they become disruptive and loud. They scream and demand and cry and manipulate. They hijack our serenity, our conversations, our emotions, and turn us into panicked humans who will do anything to appease and console and acquiesce. The mind makes us a frantic dysfunctional caregiver, too. But it is not the mind's fault, it has been trained to behave like this; it has been spoiled and allowed to behave badly. And clearly this behavior has worked because it continues to engage in it and get what it wants: control over us.

The mind learns how to navigate the world by experiencing

what does and doesn't work. What gets it what it wants and what doesn't. Which behavior is rewarded and which condemned. We have trained our minds, or more accurately, our minds have trained us. This happens so subtly, over such lengths of time, that we usually are unaware of it—or at least we choose to be.

Remember, our minds want to avoid pain, and avoiding pain usually means conforming to whatever norm is perceived around us. Different attracts attention, usually negative. Different draws criticism or rejection. The mind, thinking it is protecting us, moves away from anything different, so we slowly, seemingly unconsciously start to abandon ME for WE. We start to adopt the myths around us as our own without questioning them. Or, conversely, we rebel against the norm and against the myths.

I was teased horribly as a child and it hurt deeply. I used to be chased down the halls of my elementary school by two bullies, Scott and Todd. They loved to torment me, call me names, and make me feel afraid. I was terrified and my young mind didn't understand why being ME would draw such negative attention, so I struggled and worked to change myself, to water down my individuality, to sand away the details of my being that made me unique and special yet drew criticism—all for the purpose of not feeling the pain of being bullied. Over time, it came to feel like blending in was my full-time job. Eventually I even tried to anticipate what might draw negative attention and change it in advance. I did this until I completely lost ME in the WE of society.

And it worked. I gained acceptance. I was teased less. I became more popular. And it felt good. But the power of ME trying to express itself would not be quelled and became like a ticking time bomb battling with WE to express itself.

We can be at war with our own minds, the minds that so lovingly and carefully sought to protect us when we were vulnerable and hurt as children, but really need to step aside now that we are grown. As we become adults we have the ability to protect ourselves, however we don't override or let go of the programming that molded us because it seemingly has become us. Working to anticipate and avoid pain, judgment, and retribution daily or achieving acceptance and love or working to keep us safe and help us survive is what our minds do.

Coming into right relationship to the mind is much like taming a wild beast. We must sometimes arm ourselves with a whip and a chair, and let it know, in no uncertain terms, that it is our knowing and our essence and our unique expression of All That Is that should be bravely and authentically running our lives. How different our lives become when we are not run by irrational fear or a desire for sameness, mediocrity, and conformity!

The diamond that is your singular expression of the Universe is waiting to be emancipated from the black goo that hides its radiance—goo applied one microscopic layer at a time by the experience of living, until you eventually forgot you were the diamond within. One experience at a time, we all give away our radiance or dim it. And one experience at a time is how we can reclaim that radiance and shine again!

It is most important to know that you are not your mind. You are not the spoiled child or the wild beast. You are pure and brave and whole and wondrously unique and deeply loved. You are literally stardust that has been animated by the same breath that created all matter and lives within it.

In this moment, right now, you can experience this for yourself. It is easy and does not take years of training or decades of therapy or a certificate or a degree. It simply takes a moment of presence, a change in perspective, a waking up to see that you are not the beast or the bratty child though often we feel fused with them. You are the knowing within and beyond and beneath them. You are the lion whisperer and you are the parent that can soothe the child and make it feel safe. In every moment we have a choice as to which part of ourselves we choose to associate with, which perspective we choose to come from, and which energy we use to fuel our creations.

Here's a tool I use to awaken my sleep-creator and bring forth my conscious Creator. (Who do you think drives the bus when we sleep-create? That's right, the loud, crazy-ass, bratty child or the wild, snarling, drooling, smelly beast, that's who. And can the kid or beast drive? Hell no! Both have the attention span of a fruit fly at a picnic.) At any moment during the day (you can set an alarm on your phone or watch or computer to remind you to do this once or twice a day, or hourly, if it helps), I simply say, "STOP," and then I focus on creating a space between thoughts, an opening, a beat.

Now, trust me, the mind does not like to be shushed or interrupted, so be prepared for a bit of a battle when you first try this technique. Usually you will interrupt it when it's on a roll about this or that, or something or other, and like a spoiled child or wild beast it will try to overpower you, ignore you, attack you, or embarrass you, and then continue with what it was doing. It will test you to see just how serious you are about changing your behavior or stepping into the driver's seat of your creation bus and sending it (beast or child) to the back of the bus to sit quietly and obediently until you call on it to assist you in an appropriate action for which it was designed.

Once you've achieved a momentary reprieve from the busy and random rantings of the mind by saying (or exclaiming or screaming), "STOP" (internally or out loud), you enter into the field of pure potentiality. The field where the true YOU, the essential YOU, resides when you aren't focused and lost in all the clutter and noise of your inner and outer worlds.

Once there is silence, ask yourself: "Who is it that said, 'Stop,' and who did the stopping?" *Hmmmmm*. No, you are not schizophrenic. You are perfectly normal. But you are no longer fused with your mind either. When you step into the field, you are separated from it and experiencing the quiet as the be-er and see-er and know-er within. This is your authentic self, the self that allowed the mind to bully it into retreat in favor of sameness that would relieve you from pain or bring you praise. Only to leave you instead in the dull and ever present pain caused by the separation of you from YOU.

Reintroduce yourself to this part of yourself. Dialogue with it. Embrace it. And while you are at it, thank the child or the beast for allowing this powerful moment to happen. It's a moment in which you have reconnected with YOU.

This is HOME. The self you find here is the one that guided you to this book; it drove you to question, to seek, and to struggle against the gravitational pull of other people's stories and myths. It is like a giant lotus flower. It can do nothing but bloom beautifully, for this is what it was created to do! It will bloom whether or not you like it or want it. And it is, right now!

Now that you have come home, I suggest you do whatever it takes to get out of the way of your true self on a more permanent basis so that it can do what it so perfectly and brilliantly was designed to do.

Now that you have been reintroduced to YOU, it will be harder and harder to let the spoiled child and the ferocious beast get their way. But get their way they will. It may get ugly before it gets easier. The lunatics have been running the asylum for as long as you can remember and they are not going to take kindly to a shift in power. They will fight and cajole and demand and get loud. Trust me, mine did.

I was shocked by the lengths to which my child and beast went to stay in control of my vehicle. For me letting my true self take over was a battle. Like training a dog or raising a child, it took consistency and commitment and perseverance and discipline for me to train my mind. But it doesn't have to. That was my path.

For some people, once they experience the I within and beneath the mind, that's it. It's curtains for the child and the beast. *Poof,* they are gone. Your experience will be your own experience. I only give you one suggestion to ease your path, and that is to have fun with it as much as possible. Don't get all stern and serious about this shit. Don't turn yourself into one of those parents that bark the same commands over and over and over and are continuously ignored by their children. Those kinds of parents look all kinds of crazy. Play with this and laugh at yourself and at your mind. Laugh at the baby, walk away, and leave it to its tantrum. Laugh at the charging beast. Make it a game.

None of us needs more seriousness in our lives, NONE! All of us could stand to have a little more levity and more whacky, silly fun! So when your mind acts out, talk to it like a child, tell it you see it and that you know what it's up to. Pull down its pants and give it a good, swift, bare-bottomed spanking right in public, like you mean it.

Don't worry, no one will arrest you or report you or shame you on Facebook for spanking your mind child!

Or if the beast roars and charges, and sends you scrambling for cover beneath old, irrational fears, crack the whip and drive it back with a chair until it sits quietly on its seat, purring like a kitten. No animal rights activist group is going to shut down your circus for this, although maybe someone should have shut it down a long time ago.

If the child and beast approaches don't resonate with you, find whatever framework or game works for you and play with that. Sometimes I name all the different hijackers that take over my vehicle and I dialogue with them. I view them as being my own internal version of the seven dwarfs from the story of Snow White. Let's see there's Bitter and Grouchy and Bossy and Angry and Vic-Timmy and Give-Uppy and T-Pity. Do whatever works to help you retrain your mind ("Sit. Stay. Good mind!"), so that the YOU you have reconnected with between thoughts, the authentic YOU, is in the driver's seat of your creation bus. When you do this, and the more you do this, you will experience the ease of your life blooming inside you and outside you, and others will notice and you will inspire by example.

And remember, once the child or beast or dwarf is quiet, praise it for listening, love it, embrace it, dance with it, talk to it in a silly voice, and show it that it has nothing to fear when you, the real YOU, the stardust-wrapped spark of creation, commands your vehicle and begins the journey home to YOU!

OH MY. I just got a visual of my creation bus sputtering down the road with "Brad's Three-Ring Circus" painted on the side with pictures of the dwarfs, the child, and the lion in bright colors. Music is blazing and all are singing along, with an occasional "HI HO, HI HO, it's off to HOME we go" tossed into the mix. Kinda like the bus in The Adventures of Priscilla, Queen of the Desert, but without the boas and dresses.

Well, OK, maybe one of the dwarves isn't a dwarf at all, but a big, proud, beautiful, confident, smart, sassy black woman named Mabel. Because what gay man doesn't have a beautiful, powerful black woman inside him running the show once in a while? And lord, she don't travel light. That woman's got more shoes and wigs and hats and accessories than the good lord knows what to do with!

Only silly humans are allowed on my clown bus. *Mmmmm-KAY! Snap!*

CHAPTER THIRTEEN

HELP, I'VE BEEN HIJACKED!

*Being hijacked is an opportunity to free ourselves
from the entanglement of our wounds.*

Ever notice how sometimes, seemingly out of nowhere, you are hijacked into an extreme emotional state of anger or fear or anxiety or depression? It seems we are always taken to the challenging, uncomfortable end of the emotional spectrum. (It's like *The Invasion of the Body Snatchers.*) Why can't we be hijacked instead into joy or deep satisfaction? Alas, that has not been my experience. Usually I am hijacked by strong emotions that physically overwhelm me. And once in this state, they take over my body and mind and have a way of saying and doing things that I usually regret later on. Or they just keep me in an uncomfortable state that impacts the quality of my thoughts, words, and actions and therefore my creation. Then, I stay in that state until some catalytic event occurs or until I am able to do a hard reset that brings me out on the other side, like a good night's sleep.

Regardless, I'm confident we all know how this feels.

I found myself on the other side of one of these hijacking episodes apologizing to myself or someone else for my behavior so many times that finally, after it happened one too many times, I decided to examine WTF was going on, and what I discovered changed my life forever. It's funny how a little conscious reflection or self-examination can do that sometimes (and why most of us don't do this more often is beyond me). What I found upon deeper examination was that each of these moments was an opportunity for healing. What was actually happening was that an old wound and emotional energy stored with it were being triggered by an external event that my mind or the wounded part of me experienced as similar to the event that created the original wound. When this happens, all the emotions I stuffed down when I got wounded come flooding forth as if I'd struck oil. Black crude shoots into the air and nothing can be done to get the well of emotion under control until the pressure subsides. I have felt this same way over and over again. But once I realized what was actually happening, I developed some tools to deal with the eruptions of crude emotion more consciously, which I would like to share with you now.

If/when this happens to you, the first and most important thing to do is to realize that it is happening. Realize that you've been hijacked by an event that has triggered a deep and powerful emotional response in you. Realizing you've been hijacked will separate you from the mind's machinations and you'll find that the realizer, the deeper part of you, can actually rationally witness the emotional hijacker and negotiate with it so that it does not do the same amount of damage that it once would have.

Now, when it happens to me, I literally say to myself, "HELP, I've been hijacked!" (Remember, we wanna have fun with this stuff.) And once the realizer in me is aware, I take conscious steps to contain the damage OR seize on the healing opportunity that is being presented and do some deep inner work.

Once I've separated myself from the hijacker and am witnessing the emotional beast that has taken possession of my vehicle, one course of action I can take is to quarantine the beast. This basically means to remove it from circumstances, places, and situations where it will speak and act from its activated place. It is essential to do this, because, as we've all experienced, we are not rational in this state. We do not say or do rational things in this state so quarantine is a means of damage control.

The power you feel when you wake up in the middle of one of these episodes is incredible because you can experience the dialogue between two parts of yourself. The deepest truest part of who you are, your authentic, unwavering, loving, true self, your awakened Creator can hold incredible conversations with your wounded self, the sleep-creator. This alone is healing and cathartic, but it's just the beginning.

Then you can actually shift control to the awakened creator, who can then make rational decisions and choose NOT to make a mess of reality from the unbalanced place of temporary insanity. (Sometimes this will take every ounce of energy and consciousness you can muster while you are under attack from the hijacker.) You know what I'm speaking of when I say making a mess, right? It's the mess of a voice mail or an email or a text that the next day makes you cringe and which you'd give your first-born child to take back. Yep, those messes. So, to avoid those messes, either physically quarantine the beast by removing yourself to a safe place like your car, room, or office, or stepping outside and taking a walk or a run, or going to get a cup of coffee or whatever. Whatever you can do to physically separate yourself so that the hijacker doesn't say or do something you will regret, do that.

You can also quarantine the beast wherever you are by just speaking to it and calling out the truth. You can say, "I have been 'hijacked.' An old wound has been activated and I choose to not let the activation drive (and likely crash) my bus (AGAIN). Instead I am putting my conscious self in the driver's seat so that I can be hyper-aware of what I do and say next, so that I am doing and speaking consciously rather than letting my wounds speak for me."

Quarantining is calling the awakened creator forth in each of us and putting it in the driver's seat while moving the sleep creator to the passenger seat so that we can choose differently, be differently, create differently, and bring more conscious creation to our lives. This will not be easy at first. Trust me, when I first realized that I could do this, that I could WAKE UP within an episode, I was amazed. EVEN SO, I often lost the battle. The hijacker would win and I would be consumed by emotion. I would say and do things that literally felt like an insane person was doing them.

The best example of this is road rage. In a state of road rage, people are not rational; they've been hijacked by anger and powerlessness and act as if they've become possessed by monsters.

This is what temporary insanity is all about.

Once the hijacking has played itself out, our consciousness returns to see the havoc and wreckage that is the result of our temporary insanity. Then the clean up must begin. Sometimes there are consequences for what we've said or done that we cannot take back. I truly believe that our prisons are predominantly populated by people who lost this battle and did something really messy that was also considered illegal. This is one unfortunate end of the spectrum of the consequences of hijacking. The other end of the spectrum is that we didn't do much damage and can return to our normal state without being asked to pay a penalty. Regardless of what we "wake up" to after one of these hijacking episodes, what we need to realize right now, together, is that we ultimately have a CHOICE: We can choose to be awakened creators.

So back to our quarantined beast . . . Just like a geyser, the pressure and intensity of feeling will subside with the passage of time or if we do something to release it, like run or scream or sleep. All these help us reset ourselves to our original state in which we can create rationally. Quarantining is one of the tools I developed for myself, and the more you use it, the more you will experience and understand that what is happening is not YOU. There is a you beneath the hijacking that can witness and even take control of the situation. This YOU is your authentic self, an awakened creator, and it is always there waiting for you to call it forth. Doing so is like exercising a muscle: The more you do it, the stronger it gets and the more consciously you will create your life.

"But what if my attempts at quarantining don't work," you say? Well, oftentimes, in the beginning of this work for me, it didn't. The hijacker was just too unruly and powerful, and the emotions were too strong for me to rationalize with them or contain them. When this happened, I would force myself to take immediate responsibility for whatever I said or did while possessed by the hijacker.

A good example of taking radical responsibility for my hijacker took place on a checkout line at a Whole Foods Market.

I felt annoyed and impatient and angry. Basically, the primary emotion was anger, which created my state of annoyance and impatience with everything and everyone. This literally tainted my reality—ALL OF IT! Well, the line wasn't moving fast enough and the checkout lady, in my current state, seemed to be an idiot. One thing to note is that I truly believed she was an idiot and inept at her job (that is how strongly the hijacking beast warps and manipulates our reality), so when I got to the front of the line I treated her like an idiot. I was short with her. I didn't smile. I didn't say hello. And I made an unkind comment to her, the specifics of which I cannot recall. The point here is that in my activated state my sleep-creator was creating, and as a result what I was creating was hurt and pain and suffering.

If I had left it like that, then this poor woman might then have created all day from a place of being hurt or angry and a chain reaction would be set off. I couldn't have that.

I got all the way to my car before the hijacker stepped back, satiated by his cruelty, and I was able to call forth the awakened creator in me to quickly assess the damage and decide what to do about it. The second tool that I use in situations such as these is radical responsibility. Radical responsibility in this situation meant owning what I'd said and how I'd behaved and going back to clean up the mess that the ugly, raging beast had created.

I walked back into the store and up to the lovely, sweet checkout girl (now that I was perceiving the world from my high-est place, I could see her beauty) and I apologized. I looked her in the eye and said, "I am so sorry for treating you unkindly. I was having a tough day and I treated you unkindly, and that hurt me. I want you to know that I am deeply and truly sorry, because you didn't deserve it, and I am asking for your forgiveness. (No details or story are needed about what a "tough day" is. In fact, don't go into the drama or details, as no one needs or wants that and it's irrelevant in the present moment.)

What happened next was magical. The checkout girl burst into tears and thanked me profusely. She said that my apology was the nicest thing anyone had ever done for her. Of course, then I burst into tears, too, and there we were, crying together in Whole Foods Market. Both of us were forever changed in that moment because I cleaned up my mess. I took responsibility for the havoc the beast had wreaked in my life. And it was knowing that I had made a commitment to always make myself clean it up and take responsibility that helped me wake up in this situation and prevent future damage when in a hijacked state.

By the way, radical responsibility is a tool that actually makes me better at quarantining because I DO NOT LIKE cleaning up messes and taking radical responsibility for my hijacker doesn't always end in a magical moment. Sometimes cleaning up a mess ends with someone telling me that I'm a terrible person. *OUCH!* Or an asshole, or whatever. Regardless, I always take my licks. I take responsibility for my actions and whatever the response, to me it feels GOOD because I know that my awakened creator is getting more time in the driver's seat. Slowly and quietly the quality of my life is changing and my awakened creator is growing stronger.

The third tool for coping with being hijacked, and probably the most powerful, yet complex and challenging of them all is the *emotional purge.* When I realized that what was happening during a hijacking was that an old wound was being triggered, and saw how an opportunity for healing was being presented, I wanted to get to the bottom of things and understand what the original wound was. I wanted to take advantage of the valuable opportunity for deep healing. Emotional purging can only be done when you have the time and are in a place where you can do a deeper dive into the pain of the old wounds, so for me this is usually only possible when I am at home.

Here's what I do. The catalytic moment occurs: Some- one says or does something to set me off. Then I have the awareness that I've been hijacked and say, "Help, I've been hijacked." Then I let myself be consumed by the emotions that come pouring forth. (Again, I am seeing the image of striking oil and a dirty, gooey, messy, smelly stream of crude emotion shoots uncontrollably fifty-plus feet into the air.) I lie down and let the emotion come. This allows much of the unexpressed emotion associated with the original wound to be released. *Warning: This is not a comfortable process.*

The first time I got the message to do this and did it, I understood why we humans engage in certain behaviors like drinking alcohol, exercising, having sex, binge eating, and so forth, to help us numb out and avoid having to deal with these powerful and uncomfortable emotions. Because just sitting and experiencing the geyser of emotions was almost unbearable. What was fascinating and magical about the experience, however, is that I got to witness that I am NOT my emotions. Emotions are just sensations, they are chemical reactions. If we identify with them, they can consume us and govern our thoughts, words, and actions. If simply witnessed, we realize that they are just energy that was stored and unexpressed during some powerful experience, usually one that we perceived as negative or traumatic.

I started using this tool more and more frequently and being in the geyser so that I could purge as much of the stored, trapped goo from my past as possible. In the process, I discovered that once the repressed emotion is let out there is nothing left to trigger in the future. There is no well of unexpressed emotion that need explode forth into our present life if it has been given a chance to express itself. And I noticed this as I went about living and something would happen that would normally trigger me and . . . NOTHING. I would literally say to myself, *Wow, that really used to bother me and now nothing happens. Ahhhhhh, freedom.*

But wait, there's more, and you can go even deeper into healing. While sitting in an explosion of emotion—sometimes sadness, sometimes anger, sometimes anxiety—I would ask my wise, knowing self to reveal the source event underneath the emotion. When I did this the first time, a whole new world of deep healing was revealed to me. During these emotional purging sessions I was taken to memories I hadn't thought about in years or decades. The connection to the source event was almost instantaneous once I asked for it to be revealed.

Sometimes you may need to keep asking, or if you are not ready to fully release both the emotion AND event, then the memory may not come to mind. If you have endured trauma, you may wish to get support from a mental health professional. Early on, I benefitted greatly from the wisdom and experience of these professionals. They helped me learn to navigate these otherwise dark and scary realms. By all means trust yourself and if feels too big and too scary then get help. Remember, we cannot do this thing called life alone!

Here's what I personally have come to believe: It is my experience that if a particular well of emotion associated with a particular event has been triggered then we ARE ready to heal it. We are ready to release it. It is by design. Through emotional purging, we can take full advantage of an emotional hijacking to do deep healing. Our bodies and awakened creators are wise beyond measure, and they would never point us to a memory or emotional reservoir through a catalytic event (hijacking) that we were not ready to heal. That's why our emotions are truly our guides. They show us what needs to be released and integrated. We just need to awaken to these opportunities and move from sleep-creator to awakened creator and address them one by one.

Being hijacked is an opportunity to free ourselves from the entanglement of our wounds and the patterns, beliefs, and programs we created around them.

CHAPTER FOURTEEN

PUT IT DOWN AND LET IT GO!

*What is, is what is, regardless of the size of it,
the scale of it, the impact of it, or the level of emotions
that respond to it. It is. Period.*

Over and over, in book after book and seminar after seminar, we are told about the powerfully simple concept of *letting go* or *surrendering.* The number of books and lectures on this one topic alone is staggering. Truly. The reason so much advice exists about it is that this simple concept is THAT important and THAT powerful. It is also that easy. So why did it take me almost thirty years of hearing about it over and over, and attempting it over and over, before I could get it? Besides the fact that I'm a stubborn, silly human, I mean.

Sometimes the simplest, most powerful truths elude us the longest because we humans just LOVE to overthink, overanalyze, and overcomplicate just about everything in our lives. When I was really ready to grasp the concept of letting go and understand that I had in my possession, and had always had in my possession, the key to end all my suffering in an instant, I got it. My dear friend Tippy helped me understand. Oh thank you, Great Spirit, for the gift of Tippy, and thank me for learning to listen when it matters. It was another AHA moment for dear old Brad. Another shining example of how the Universe sprinkles tools and gifts throughout humanity so that we can find them at the perfect time and in the perfect place and be aided in our journey home to ourselves.

Maybe now is your time to understand this simple concept.

Spirit helped me get the whole concept of letting go by sending me the image of a game of tug of war. As you know, it takes two people to play tug of war and both have to choose to play (there's that choice thing again) and really commit to playing in order to make the game work. If one opponent doesn't play, the game ends.

When something, anything happens in our lives, it happens. Objectively speaking, it simply and clearly just is what is. If we could freeze the moment when it happens and examine it before our automatic response mechanism kicks in, or before our patterns or wounds or beliefs or programs respond for us, then we could enjoy having objectivity about any event or circumstance and not get swept up in a feeling or opinion.

This is a VERY powerful way to let go quickly. Simply freezing the moment keeps at bay the sleep-creator that wants to respond automatically before WE, the real US, has any real chance to awaken into consciousness and respond from wholeness to an event.

I've failed at this so many times! Seriously, I lost count at a gazillion. But when I finally got it, I got it good. When I could freeze a moment and observe an event objectively, I saw that events dangle one end of a tug of war rope in front of us, and then tease and taunt and plead with us to grab hold and engage in a struggle against whatever we think is on the other end of the rope. The struggle is fueled by our desire for reality to be something, anything, different than what it is.

It's like a comedy skit really. This same ridiculous dance happens on the smallest and the biggest of levels. Regardless of the size and impact and emotions involved, the truth remains the same: We always have a choice to accept what is and refuse to play tug of war, and if we make this choice we can avoid suffering of any kind. Because you see, what is, *is*. Period. It happened. It arrived. It landed near us or on us, even all over us, or on a friend, or on the loved one of the person behind us in the checkout line. It happened. And once a thing happens, there is nothing that you, I, or anyone else can do to change it.

Since we cannot change it or get out of the way, we have only two choices. We can accept it, adjust to it, deal with it, and move forward, or we can rage and fight and kick and scream and suffer and play tug of war with it until we are done doing so and then adjust to it, deal with it, and move forward. In the end, we will have to deal with it and we will have to make whatever adjustments are required. We have to move forward because time forces us to step into the next moment and the next. The only difference in the quality of our lives is the amount of resistance we feel to that which is. We can choose to play tug of war, or not. Since to resist is to suffer, basically we can choose either to suffer or not to suffer.

Looked at this way, why would we ever choose to suffer? That's a good question. No doubt there are infinite reasons. No doubt we are right and justified for every reason. But the base truth of human nature is that it is we who choose our own suffering. An event that has happened is. Everything after that is our choice: How we accept it. How we respond to it. How we adjust because of it. And these choices will either create ease for us or they will create suffering.

Let's move from concept to application, from the hypothetical to the practical. We'll start small so that we can ease into this technique and remain open, relaxed, and receptive rather than going into opposition mode, shutting down, and holding on tightly to our belief that the Sun revolves around the Earth. If you are already moving into this mode, then shut the book. Take a walk. Dance. Watch a movie. Let it be. Only come back when you feel ready because I really want you to get this simple concept and not take thirty years to get it like I did simply because I was stubborn and silly and wanted to be right.

Ready?

Here's the scenario: We are walking along on a hot day and get a craving for an ice cream cone or gelato or coconut bliss or sorbet (whatever version of frozen treat you can eat, and if the answer is none, then a filtered, energized ice water). To our surprise, just as we realize we desire this thing, we see a store that offers what we want. We go in and they have the perfect, most divine version of whatever it is. We get it, we pay for it, and we walk outside. Life is GOOD.

Then, just when we are about to take our first sip or lick after having gone only one or two steps down the sidewalk, *SMASH*, a young guy on a skateboard, in a hurry, talking on his cell phone, runs smack into you and your tasty treat goes flying all over you and him and the ground.

FREEZE. The choices at this point are endless. Infinite.

Your sleep-creator has probably already jumped ahead and is starting to formulate a response, right? Dangling the tug of war rope . . . taunting you. It can't help itself. It all happens so fast, doesn't it? In a FLASH!

I've have gone in every direction possible at this point after what happens. Hey, I'm forty-eight. When I was young, I got angry. That's what I did because I was angry. I cursed and spit and ranted and blamed and counterattacked all over place. I grabbed at every rope and tugged and tugged. I had to win. Be right. Until I didn't have to anymore. Eventually, I grabbed at the rope less and less because I was finally getting the point that resistance NEVER changes anything! What is still is what is, only if we play tug of war do we have to contend with an even bigger mess.

My stubbornness then gave way to wisdom. (Funny how that starts to happen way too late to avoid those initial messes.) I chose to put down my end of the rope and let go and then choose.

Do you know what's really fun? When you are able to wake up at the choice point of an event or circumstance, going in the opposite direction of what is normal or expected. Instead of screaming obscenities at the inconsiderate skateboarder who toppled our tasty treat, we could help the boarder up and even offer to buy him or her a cone, since we are going to have to buy ourselves another one anyway. That's mastery.

Recently I was tested by an experience very similar to the one above. And I was literally shocked and awed by my response—or should I say, my lack thereof. A woman spilled her full, fresh, hot latte all over my groceries on the checkout conveyer belt and I stood there and no automatic response came. I just witnessed what happened. Then, in the witnessing, I was free to choose to do whatever I wanted.

The woman braced for my response and the response of the checkout lady. I saw it on her face. Her eyes darted from mine to the checkout woman's and back again. We had none. She hurriedly apologized and started to criticize herself and declare how clumsy she was, but I simply stopped her and said, "It's OK, we've all been there—no permanent damage was done, so let's just clean this up." Then I asked the cashier if we could get the woman's latte replaced and she said, "Of course we can." Together, we all laughed and cleaned, and woman turned to me and said, "Thank you for being so kind and understanding."

I said, "You're welcome. I've really and truly been there, and I know how I wish I and others had responded, and now I was able to do just that."

I hope you are seeing that whatever happens just happens, and that when we slow down a memory of an experience so we can see it frame by frame, we can see where we have had choices although we experienced having none at the time because we were hijacked by our minds. We have the ability to accept events—even difficult and unpleasant events—with love and grace and ease, and move forward, but we also have the ability to choose to argue with reality, shake it, punish it, cry about it, rage against it, and then in a day, week, month, or year, sometimes even twenty years later, move on. Regardless of what we choose to do, know this: What happened happened. It simply is. Either immediately or eventually (or never) we accept it and move forward.

Why not stop choosing all the suffering in between, and just accept what is and move on? If you can do this, and the more you can master this, the lighter and more enjoyable, steady, fun, and easy your life will be. I have had the best six months of my life at forty-eight mostly due to the fact that I stopped struggling with what is. Now I accept events as quickly as possible and then choose a course of action that creates the least amount of suffering for me and others. Until I don't. Then I suffer and cause suffering, after which I clean it up.

Ask me to tell you about the monster within me that reared

its ugly head at the Enterprise car rental counter in Melbourne, Florida, sometime. When I finally regained my sanity, I was like, "Oh no you didn't," but oh yes I did.

Or the time my friend Tippy rear-ended my brand-new car that didn't even have the license plates on it yet, and we jumped out, braced for whatever response might come, and burst into uncontrollable laughter at the ridiculousness of it. We hugged each other and people were like, "You both are crazy!"

To this kind of comment, I would hope we'd all answer, "A bit, yeah! Duh! I'm here, aren't I? On Earth. Being human. Flying blind. Crashing my creation bus. Yearning, trying, seeking. So yeah, I think *crazy* is implied."

Back to putting it down and letting it go. We worked with some simple, low-level examples above to help understand the concept at work at the most basic level. "Well, that is all good and fine," you might say. "But what about rape or cancer or muggings or murder? How do we accept what is then? These 'what ises' aren't spilled lattes or fallen ice cream cones."

To which I'd say "You are right, they are not. They are bigger events. Potentially scary events, painful events, traumatic events." I was mugged once in San Francisco. It was terrifying. I was maybe twenty, in college, and there for the UCLA vs. Stanford game. A group of young men targeted me and my friends as we were walking home from a restaurant and chased us down. I literally thought I was going to die. I thought they were going to pull out a knife and stab me and that would be that. In the end they only took my shoes. But I was in shock afterward. I'd never been the sudden victim of an unexpected crime before and literally thought that this was it—game over. But I responded typically—with fear and an overwhelming fight-or-flight response.

Later, I thought about how I would have liked to respond or how I might respond in the future should something similar happen. Perpetrators expect and feed off our fear, and normally we can't help giving it to them. But what would it have been like if I had laughed? Or what if I had stripped down naked and handed over to them everything I owned that was on me at that moment and said, "Whatever is mine is yours, please take it!" Or what if I had started to sing and just kept singing no matter what? It would have changed everything. There would have been less trauma and I would probably have had a better chance of surviving than if I fought them or feared them.

The point is that we have endless choices and yet we customarily let the choice choose us.

Some people get cancer and they are the victims of it and die as victims of it. Some get cancer and it enlivens their spirit and they smile and they fight on. Whether they survive or succumb—do you see the difference the choice makes in the quality of their lives? In no way am I judging anyone. I am just very interested in how to have a positive experience of my life no matter what outer circumstances are occurring. That's a conversation that I think is important for all of us to have with one another. Letting go helps us to maintain our equanimity in the face of challenging circumstances.

I don't expect anyone to start mastering this simple concept by starting with the big events or what would be the equivalent of a Ph.D.-level calculus equation on Day 1 of math class in first grade. Start small. Build your confidence. Build your strength. Show yourself the choices you have by playing with what is, laughing at what is, and singing when what is happens. And when and if you won't let go, don't. Be hijacked. Play tug of war until you are all muddy and you vomit. Then forgive yourself quickly and prepare for a new opportunity.

In this game, you can't strike out, so swing away! If you don't swing at the ball, you can't get a hit.

All kidding aside, please know this: What is, is what is, regardless of the size of it, the scale of it, the impact of it, or the level of emotions that respond to it. It is. Period. When we have truly mastered this concept, then no event, big or small, can pull us off our center and distract us from the truth "I am GOD and I am in charge of my emotions, my life, and my creation always and in all ways."

If you are still scratching your head or if you are pissed off at me or are just thinking, *Hunh?* then when you are ready this concept will find you again and the tools you need will find you through some other human who has the gift just for you when and as you need it.

CHAPTER FIFTEEN

CAN'T VS. WON'T

The Universe originally may have said,
"I won't" or "I don't want to," but eventually it said,
"I will," and it did, because here we are.

Please stop saying you *can't,* because that's a lie. We've established that:

1. You are God/Creator/Universe,
2. You have the power to choose
   and create your life, and
3. Every moment is a new opportunity
   to create what you both want and need.

If you want to be radically honest, you must say, "I *won't,*" because that is true. The meaning of "I WILL NOT" (*it's my choice*) is different than the meaning of "I CANNOT" (*I am incapable*).

You can. You are capable of taking action. You will not because you choose not to. In fact, try this for one day. Replace every "I can't" with an "I won't" because that is both radically honest and it means you are taking radical responsibility for your life. Stop making excuses for your choices. It's beneath you. Stop acting as if you aren't God in a meat suit exploring creation.

What if the Universe had said, "I can't"? Well, we could philosophically explore this for millennia, but basically if the Universe had said, "I can't," then nothing would exist. There would just be an infinite void where all creation now exists. At first the Universe may have said, "I won't" or "I don't want to," but eventually it said, "I will," and it did, and here we are! Thank WE!

If you want something different than what you've created,

you must do something different. You have to do things differently to get something different. It's really just a matter of how badly you want things to change whether or not you are willing to do what it takes. When it gets bad enough (and hopefully, long before then), you'll internalize this concept and declare that YOU CAN and YOU WILL.

If you can choose in this moment to slow down or hasten your breathing, to look left or look right, to listen near or afar, to scream or to whisper, to smile or to frown, to stand or to sit, then you have the power to choose smaller or bigger choices that will move you toward the realization of your highest purpose and potential or land you right back where you started when the alarm goes off tomorrow morning on yet another Ground Hog Day and you say, "UGH, I'm tired of this shit." Tired of what? YOUR creation.

"Dammit, another day of living this hell that I created for myself! I hate it, it sucks, I'm so unhappy, my body hurts, my boss is a jerk, my relationship sucks, I never have great sex, but I think I'll just create it again for the hell of it—literally! I think I'll CTRL C + CTRL V sleep-create the same thing for tomorrow so I can wake up, hit the alarm, and complain again."

Is anyone else seeing how ridiculous this is? Silly, silly humans!

So what do you say? Is it time yet to be YOU? To come home to yourself? To choose to create the life you've been searching for? Well, I'd say NOW is as good a time as any to start because the Universe, as always, is here now, waiting to conspire with you and support you with Its infinite resources and an army of humans to assist and lend their gifts. Please just don't say, "I can and will create a billion dollars so I never have to worry about anything again" or I'll barf! Or please don't say, "I can and I will create the perfect boyfriend or girlfriend who will love me for me even when I'm not really willing to be the ME I was born to be," or I'm sure it'll immediately give me a case of explosive diarrhea and there won't be a bathroom for miles. MESSY! Because when you do this, you are asking a Universe that knows you, knows your potential and knows what you are here to do, to give you what you *think* you want instead of what it knows you NEED.

CHAPTER SIXTEEN

WANT VS. NEED

Awakened creators never push or force, they flow.

So this whole "want vs. need" thing just might make me very unpopular because of the all the books and seminars and lectures and groups and retreats and popular movies that teach very different approaches. Learning how to get what they want is probably the one thing that people spend the most time, money, and resources on, and they keep getting the WRONG information about it, in my not-so-humble opinion.

There is a notion going around that if you align your energy (or aura or emotions or whatever) with what you want, then POOF it falls into your life! Whatever it is, no limits! If you want it badly enough, if you journal about it, vision board about it, share it, write it down and burn it, dance it, sing it, and otherwise align your being with that desire, it will manifest because "that's how the Universe works." Well, it might be how it works for some people, or for some person that I've never met, but everyone I've ever talked to or met or encountered or shared with is still trying to get the car, house, job, or relationship that they want. All they have to show for their effort is more *wanting.*

Hmmmmm . . . could it be that all these people just haven't mastered the simple "how to" rule for creating in this Universe? (Desire, align, poof!) Or could it be that something is missing from this little how-to guideline? Like . . . maybe the person that pulled it down from God knows where (and yes, thank you, I do know where) was napping when the first part of the message came through the channel. Or the tape recorder was still on that clear white strip and hadn't hit the brown part yet? Or they were so overwhelmed by the message that they missed a subsequent clarifying message? However, it was missed, it was missed because I've tried desiring and aligning with my wants, and there's never been a POOF. And millions of others have done the same with similar results.

So what's the dealio?

The secret of manifestation (*mmm-hmm*, I meant to say *secret)* is all about whether your desire is aligned with what you want AND what you NEED. Or more clearly, when desire is aligned with what you need for your own becoming and awakening and purpose—POOF! Wanting and needing are VERY different things, but most of us we tend to use these words interchangeably. Well, we need to stop. 'Cause they couldn't be more different. For example, you might truly need a car, but you don't need a *Porsche.* You might *want* one, and that is utterly fine with me, and I know it's fine with the Universe, 'cause, girl, SHE don't care! But if you are working as a bank teller or grocery clerk or in a midlevel management job (like myself), or even if you own your own small business, and you need a car, but want a Porsche, then you could be desiring and aligning for a long time and there won't be a *poof!*

If you push it and make it happen because you are super creator (awakened Creators never push or force, they flow), then you will probably put yourself in a not-so-great financial situation to do so. Even if you can drive around and say, "Look at me, I'm successful," are you? Do you feel successful? Really? Truly? Because of a car? No! You are not successful because of a car. Sorry, Charlie!

How can I say this with authority? Because I'm a human that has searched and questioned and tried and failed over and over and over again to find what I was looking for . . . happiness, success, a reprieve from the pain. If I could count up the money I've personally spent on books and seminars and retreats and therapy I could have probably bought a top-of-the-line Porsche multiple times over. YIKES. And while I did learn from every experience and I wouldn't take any of them back, because they are part of the sum total of who I am, I know now that the answers were simpler.

Who am I? I'm God.

What am I here to do? Be the best, shiniest me I can be—sing it!

And how, as God, do I create in this realm? By aligning myself with what my soul and the Universe want for me to be the best ME possible.

The Universe and your soul want for YOU what YOU need.

What we need is rarely what we think we want. When I finally gave up telling the Universe what I wanted and started asking her to bring me what I needed—then I got the POOF—that magic started FLOWING like maple syrup during a Wisconsin spring! Ease replaced struggle, and joy replaced suffering, and I started to KNOW that what unlocks the powers of creation in us and for us is when what we ask for aligns with what serves us in remembering and experiencing and coming home to US.

What we need is still wonderful and magical. It just might not be made of gold or fine Italian leather, or it might be, and whatever or however it is is perfect ALWAYS.

Trust me, when I started, I asked for all the same things that all of us do. I did. Over and over and over, and then I blamed myself for not being able to align with the desire so I could get the POOF. Until one day, I just gave up trying, exhausted by all the effort of trying to create what I wanted. Literally exhausted and depressed, and thinking, "What is wrong with me? Is my wand broken? Did I lose my mojo? Is there anybody out there?"

"Nothing," "No," "No," and, "You have no idea," were the answers.

When I finally was exhausted from trying, I gave in, gave up, breathed out, and reluctantly said, "Fine. What do YOU want for me? How can I serve the YOU within that I am trying to come home to? And how can I serve humanity and the Earth and Spirit with the gift that is my life?" I turned it completely around and admitted that I had NO IDEA what I wanted, which is why I was still searching and lost.

Fortunately, I knew who did. God/Creator/the Universe that made all there is, was, and ever will be, that's who. SHE created the infinite Universe with seemingly infinite galaxies and solar systems, and SHE created the insanely beautiful, complex, awe-inspiring little planet that our strange mammalian species calls home. With all the fascinating life forms and seasons and rain and rainbows and oceans and waves and the octopus and the platypus and tornados and a baby anything that is always cute as hell and makes our heart sing, and amoebas and flowers and bees and elephants and viruses and bacteria, and inner and outer space. SHE created it ALL. So *phew,* I'd need a cigarette and a nap after creating all that personally, dang! And a week of eating nothing, but banana cream pie! But that's just me. If SHE can create all that, then certainly SHE knows better than I do what I want and need.

Instead of wanting one more thing, I decided at last that I would simply ask her to bring me what I need to come home to me and serve HER in OUR creation. I looked to the most insanely amazing conductor of all time and promised to sing my singular note. I agreed to fill my lungs with all the air possible and belt out the song of ME.

Oooooh, baby! When I finally starting wanting like *this,* when want = need, I could feel all my spirit guides and angels and the Universe HERSELF smile and jump for joy and celebrate because NOW they could really conspire with me to make great things happen—all of which they knew would serve who I truly am and who I am becoming!

I'll be more specific in how my asking changed. Instead of praying and subjugating myself to a "greater power" compared to whom we rarely feel worthy, I declared my knowing that I AM GOD. (I even told Siri to call me God on my iPhone, so that when emails come to my computer they are addressed to God! It's true! And I love it! FUN FUN FUN.)

I told the Universe, "I AM God and I have at my disposal all the powers of creation.

"I am a drop and I am the ocean.

"I am a unique, singular expression of the Universe and I happen to be called Bradley Robert Thomason in this here and now."

To this SHE responded, "Yes and bravo." Then she asked,

"What can I do for you, oh beautiful, perfect Bradley Robert Thomason?"

To which I responded, "No, what can I do for you? How can I shine my essence brighter in service to OUR creation? Please help me to remember, so that the purest essence of who I am can reemerge and shine without obstruction, embarrassment, regret, or judgment."

Her answer? "Now you're talking."

Now when I create, I first identify a need (a place to live, a professional engagement, a car, a relationship . . . or whatever). I mean a NEED. Meaning I'm moving so I *need* a new place to live. Meaning my lease is expiring so I *need* a new car. Meaning my current job is coming to an end so I *need* a new one that pays me enough to continue to live comfortably or more than comfortably. These are real needs.

Here is the beautiful part. I put absolutely no limits on what the fulfillment of the need looks like. I don't ask specifically for either a Porsche or a Hyundai. I don't ask for a mansion or a broken-down studio apartment in the bad part of town. I don't ask to be CEO and I don't ask to be the janitor. I don't ask for the most beautiful, perfect blond-haired (or brunette or redheaded) 10 and I don't ask for someone, anyone, just to keep me from being lonely. I ask HER to bring me the "PERFECT DIVINE" living space, relationship, work opportunity, car, companion, or whatever. The "PERFECT DIVINE" one! I own that request and I demand it be answered because I need it!

Thus far, what has been delivered to me is ALWAYS more perfect, more beautiful, and more what I want AND need than I could ever have imagined for myself. EVER! To this day I have never been let down. The Universe has always delivered. Well, SHE and the minion of angels and guides who work with US. (Love you all, my friends. Thanks for the good work, keep it up!).

Now, I'm going to caution you against running out and simply trying this until you are ready, and here's why: The Universe speaks through subtle messages, images, inspirations, and synchronicities, and you have to be attuned to these to know when to turn right or left, or make a phone call or act, or wait and be patient. Perfect Divine does not happen in our time, it happens in HERS. That's part of why it is always perfect and divine. ALWAYS. Without exception.

We humans . . . we silly, silly humans . . . especially in the western world, want things NOW. We want them how we want them, and we like to be very specific about how we want them. Ever overheard someone ordering a latte at Starbucks or a salad at your favorite restaurant . . . "Substitute this, less of that, more of that, with this on the side . . ."? There's nothing wrong with any of this specificity, but remember, what we *want* is not always what we truly *NEED.* So one of the things we need is to learn to let go of knowing. (Oooh, this is a hard one). Let go of needing, let go of wanting, and simply trust that the power that created the heavens and the Earth is at work on your behalf and then go about your business and "listen" with your whole being.

Listening with your whole being is like dancing with the Divine. You have to let HER lead, *duh!* And you definitely can't think. You've just gotta flow, baby, flow, and feel, baby, feel, with your heart and your whole being. SHE is doing her best to guide you right to what you are asking her for and it will be the perfect divine version of what you need.

I have numerous, powerful stories about how perfectly and beautifully the request for the "perfect divine _____" works although I only discovered and started to use *perfect divine* as a tool after exhausting myself with all my wanting. Until then I felt like a failure at creating. Finally I had no alternative but to let go and allow a power greater than me show me what it wanted for me (which is what I needed). Are you starting to pick up what I'm putting down?

I tried various versions that preceded *perfect divine* until I landed on *perfect divine* and knew with certainty that I had it, the best way to ask the Universe, my soul, my guides, and the angels to work their miracles for me and my highest good.

In 1996, I was living in New York City. My company had just moved me there to fill a new position. To start off, they put me in an apartment on the Upper-Upper East Side, in a building called Normandy Court, which was on the corner of Third Avenue and

Normandy. It was a perfectly fine place to live, and most importantly, it took dogs. I had moved to the City with my beautiful dog, Brooks, a border collie/golden retriever mix whom I adopted while living in Aspen, Colorado, after graduating college. The building was blocks from Central Park, perfect for walking around the Reservoir in the mornings and evenings. But I only had a short-term lease on the apartment, for something like three months, after which I could either stay there or find a new apartment.

Now, as anyone who has lived in NYC knows, the Upper-Upper East Side can be quite far from anyplace fun and hip in the city (at least in 1996), so it was my plan to move downtown and closer to my office when my lease was up. With this intention, I began daily to ask Spirit to bring me the perfect divine apartment in New York City. That's all! I didn't ask for a studio or a one-bedroom. I did not ask for a particular building or neighborhood. I left the request simply as "perfect divine" and I asked for this every day, sometimes over and over again. I would thank the Universe for bringing my new apartment to me without effort and with perfect ease, and I waited, and I waited.

Six weeks until moving day turned into three weeks, then two weeks. I began to think I was suffering from some kind of delusion that this would actually happen, but still I waited and relaxed and let it go and I trusted HER. I did not search in the paper, and I did not walk the streets looking for FOR RENT signs. I did, however, tell people I was looking for an apartment in order to activate my network (since we can't do it alone).

I waited and remained hyper attuned to my inner guidance and waited for the voice of the Universe to guide me to my perfect divine apartment. Meanwhile, friends said I was crazy, that I would never just find an apartment in New York without pounding the pavement and working at it diligently. And with a full-sized dog, forget it! "Impossible," they said.

Well, one night, I was on the Upper West Side at a bar grabbing a drink when a group of people struck up a conversation with me. They asked me where I was from and I told them California. Over the next couple of hours, we exchanged polite conversation.

At the end of this conversation, one of them invited me to a party he was having the following week. He said it might be a good place for me to meet new people since I was still only a couple of months new to the City.

Fast forward to a week later. I had forgotten about the party and was lying in bed on the Upper East Side in my studio apartment. I was literally under the covers and in my underwear, when something said, loudly, "GET UP AND GO TO THE PARTY!"

I remember it vividly still. The voice in my head was loud enough to make me sit up.

And then my brain kicked in and started rationalizing the command. *Get up? Now? And what, get dressed and go all the way from the Upper-Upper East Side to the Upper-Upper West Side? What's that gonna cost us?*

There's no subway and no direct route to get there. You have to go over, down, and around, and back up. It would be at least a $20 cab ride both there and back, and I was not making a lot of money at the time.

I listened to my brain and lay back down and prepared to fall asleep when I heard it again. "GET UP AND GO TO THE PARTY!" It is rare that I hear a communication so clearly and unmistakably, so after this second booming command I decided I had no choice but to get up and start the journey westward. All the while of course, my bratty inner child was complaining and saying things like, "This had better be worth it" or "I had better at least meet the man of my dreams at this stupid party."

I got dressed, freshened up, brushed my teeth, and started out for the party. I took a cab and arrived at around 11:30 PM, which in New York is early for most gatherings. I went into the party and I was like, *WHAT? I got outta bed for this?* I was the new, lonely guy who showed up alone, knowing no one. I grabbed a glass of something to lubricate my social awkwardness and disguise my disappointment and make the best of it. I chatted here and listened there until I found myself talking to one of the guys I had met at the bar. It was a pleasant conversation. He asked me what I did, how I liked New York, and all the other usual questions. I responded politely and inquired about what he did. Then he asked me where I was living and I said Normandy Court on the Upper-Upper East Side, but that I was hoping to move.

Hearing this, he smiled and said, "Well, I have two apartments on hold right now. One is in Chelsea and the other is in Hell's Kitchen. I was going to let the one in Chelsea go tomorrow because I ultimately decided I wanted to find a roommate and the apartment in Hell's Kitchen is a two-bedroom. Maybe you'd like Chelsea."

I said, "Wow, that'd be great."

My new friend told me to give him my number and said he would call me the next day right after he phoned to let the Chelsea apartment go, so that I could be the first to see it. And call he did. And off I went to see the apartment. It was a one-bedroom apartment in Chelsea on Sixteenth Street close to Seventh Avenue, a perfect location. It was also rent stabilized and in a pre-war building with high ceilings and big windows in each room overlooking a garden next door, so there was lots of light, AND, wait for it, they took dogs. "No problem," the landlord said. This apartment became my home for the next five years. From 1996–2001 I lived there with Brooks and paid under $1000/month rent.

When it was time for me to move back to California in 2001 (informed by yet another booming voice saying that it was time to leave, two months before 9/11), the building management paid me $15,000 to move because they wanted me out so that they could upgrade the unit and break the rent stabilization restrictions. OH YEAH, PERFECT DIVINE. The gift that keeps on giving.

I am not special. I am no different or more gifted or more knowing than any of you reading these words. I simply learned to stop telling (or screaming at) the Universe what I wanted and instead I gave HER the freedom to create things for me that were better and more perfect than I could ever have imagined myself.

I also learned to listen to synchronicity, to subtle signs, and to whisperings (and sometimes the booming voice), and used them to guide myself with my whole instrument instead of just with my mind (which always had reasons why I could not trust, or I was crazy, or deluded or plain stupid). I kindly disciplined my mind, and I experienced miracles as a result . . . great, big, perfect, divine miracles.

To take this a step further. When I am truly being led by the Universe in HER dance and have given HER permission to bring me what I need when I need it, I will find that before I even awaken to the realization that I need something, it is delivered effortlessly by the Universe just when I end up needing it. Like feeling the pang of hunger that tells you that your body needs to be fed when simultaneously you notice that you are standing next to an apple tree with perfectly ripened apples on it. Then, when you reach for the one apple that caught your eye that is slightly out of reach, it falls into your hand. And that, my friends, is what lies even beyond perfect divine when we are so in the flow and aligned with the Universe and our purpose and potential that things come to us as if by magic just when we need them and in a way that is bigger and better and more perfect than we could ever imagine.

CHAPTER SEVENTEEN

TEACH A MAN TO FISH

The Universe says, "Girl, don't look at me.
It's your mess. You clean it up."

Through trial and error, I've discovered that there's a little more to the business of cocreation with the Universe than just clarifying our wants vs. needs and asking for the perfect divine version of something. Let's call this the "Teach Me to Fish" clause in the *How to Create the Life You Want* manual.

Sometimes we create a mess for ourselves in a specific area of life, whether that mess is relationship related, health related, work related, money related, or whatever related doesn't really matter. The key thing in this scenario is that we just don't want to clean up the mess we made because we know how much effort and time it will take. It's kind of like the day when I was making a super green shake. I put in some fresh-squeezed lemon juice, some super green powder, some raw, organic, fair-trade cacao powder, some raw, organic, fair-trade maca powder, a raw egg from my own free-range chickens (*mmm-mmmm*, love my girls), some almond milk, and a little maple syrup to add some sweetness to my sweetness! After I put all these goodies in my Ninja blender, I got busy busy busy, buzzing around my kitchen, and (you know what's coming, right?) then I whipped around and hit the ᴏɴ button to blend it all up without noticing that I had forgotten to put the lid on the blender. *KAPLOWEE*, my green shake exploded all over the kitchen. I mean, it was on the ceiling, the floor, the cabinets, and me. It was dripping down the walls and oozing its way between the counter and the stove. Yep, that kinda mess. And I just stood there dripping in healthy goodness, frozen, thinking, "That did not just happen. Please, someone hit rewind so I can put the lid on it."

Luckily I was in a good place that morning so instead of the normal string of profanity I would have exclaimed on another day, I just laughed and went about cleaning up the mess. I think I even went and looked at myself in the mirror just to see how messy and ridiculous I looked. And I thought, "Now I gotta clean this mess up, 'cause it ain't gonna clean itself up."

Oh, and there was also the time I left the water running into the plugged sink while I went down to investigate the cackles of a potential chicken emergency, only to come back to my kitchen flooded and water leaking down into the basement.

On both of these occasions I wished someone or something would just come and clean the mess up for me. But no one did. It was up to me.

So I cleaned. I pulled out the rags and the mop and the cleaning supplies, and before you know it, the mess went bye-bye, kitchen cleaned. What I discovered is that the cleanup is never as bad as I think it's going to be when I'm first frozen in the aftermath of making the mess. My mind usually exaggerates the enormity of the undertaking and makes it seem insurmountably big so that it can really get me invested in the drama and resistance of what needs to be done.

Well, creating messy relationships, health issues, financial complications, and work crises one thought, word, and action at a time is viewed similarly by the Universe as we view blender explosions, backing your car through a closed garage door, putting a red shirt into a white load of laundry, or spilling a perfectly sweetened, perfect cream-to-coffee ratio cup of coffee onto your laptop keyboard. The Universe says, "Girl, don't look at me. It's your mess. You clean it up." And why do you think SHE does this? Ours is a loving, perfect, all-knowing, all-powerful Universe. Why doesn't SHE just clean up our messy relationship, our health issue, our finances, or our shitty job? Because if SHE did it for us, we'd just do the same things all over again. And again. And again. A child rescued from its mistakes will never learn how to do things differently and better and take responsibility.

Our dear sweet Mother Universe is like the best parent ever. She lets us fall down and she lets us pick ourselves up again. She allows us to burn our hands on the hot stove despite her many warnings so that we can learn for ourselves what "hot" is.

So here's what you need to do to enact the "Teach Me to Fish" clause. You know the adage, right? "Give a man a fish and he eats for a day. Teach a man to fish and he eats for the rest of his life." If you survey your creation and find a particular area of it that always seems to be a mess, an area where, try as you may, you just can't seem to get it together, that's where you need to focus.

See the mess. Contemplate the gooey, sticky explosion that is all over you and possibly all over others who were standing too close to you when you created this mess. Then, ask the all-powerful, loving Universe for help. Although the Universe will not clean up your mess for you, SHE will connect you to the people or experts or teachers that can help empower you to clean up your mess, turn this piece of your creation around, and move it in the direction of your heart's desire. That way you won't make this particular mess again.

Ask for the Perfect Divine Help and it will come perfectly and with divine timing.

For me, the area of my life that seems to always be in a mess is my finances. Ever since I can remember, I've just been bad at managing money. So much so, that I haven't allowed myself to have a credit card in over ten years. If I have little, I manage with little. If I have a lot, I expand into a lot. I never save. Easy come, easy go. At forty-eight, while I had no consumer debt to speak of, I owed a shit ton of money to the IRS for unpaid taxes. And OH, how I prayed for the Universe to just let me win the lottery so I could pay off my taxes. I deserved it. I had been so good serving HER and giving her the gift of ME. I shouldn't have to struggle to clean up the mess, right? And lord knows I WANTED to win the lottery.

By the way, I'm still doing it actually. Just yesterday I bought a lottery ticket when I filled up with gas and I thought, "I just want to pay off my damned taxes so I don't go to debtors' prison where I'm sure I'd be very popular." Every time I ask HER to clean up my mess, she looks at me over her reading glasses, folding over the page of the section of the *New York Times* she's reading so she can make eye contact, purses her lips, cocks her head, and says, "You know where we keep the mop and bucket and cleaning supplies. Now, get to it and clean up your own damned mess."

Just this week, I did finally that. I reached out into my personal and professional networks and asked for recommendations of experts who might be able to help me learn how to help myself. I asked for the perfect divine someone who could help me learn how to master these bizarre things called *money* and *finances.* And as soon as I asked, the answers came. Then I picked up the phone and started to clean up my mess.

In the area of finances, I am like a hungry man asking for food. Money, like it or not, fair or not, is the currency of exchange in our world, which means we are required to have some basic knowledge and ability to transact with it. But instead of giving this hungry man a fish to feed his hunger, the loving, benevolent Universe insisted that I learn how to fish so that I would never go hungry again! Bless her big heart!

CHAPTER EIGHTEEN

YOUR SPACESUIT

Your body is a walking miracle.

During our adventures on Earth, we are fortunate to inhabit one of the most spectacularly complex biological creations in the known universe: the human body. The more I learn about the spacesuit that allows my spirit to explore and partake of the offerings of this realm, the more I am astounded that I actually wake up every day and have the life of a human being. The things the body is able to do simultaneously boggle the mind. In fact, it is not possible for the conscious mind to know or comprehend the complex electrical, chemical, and biological functions that go on in any given second.

As it makes its way through a seemingly ordinary day, the body is literally always doing something like a trillion functions (since I'm not a scientist, I'm going to exaggerate for effect): monitoring, responding, adjusting, anticipating, reacting, and stabilizing our systems and whole organism. ORDINARY?! The fact that we can walk and smell and see and hear and feel (physically and emotionally), and taste and sense (on a deeper level besides the basic five senses), and have a conversation or learn or play an instrument while these trillions of impulses are firing away is a MIRACLE. There is nothing ordinary about any second in our day. Every second we draw breath, we need to be thanking the Earth and the Universe for creating the perfect, beautiful, strong, resilient, self-healing, self-repairing spacesuits we're wearing that allow the pieces of God within us to explore OUR creation and create within it!

Please stop for a moment and let this sink in: Your body is a walking miracle. Literally billions of years of refinement and evolution went into creating this spacesuit. I'm sure there was trial and error along the way, and I do believe that evolution and creation conspired, and then voila—KA BAM, KA PLOWEE—ladies and gentlemen, I give you the human body!

We should build a monument or center or museum or something that showcases the human body as the brilliant and profound artistic and scientific achievement that it is. Alas we don't have one yet. Maybe I'll create one. Because seriously, it's just unfair not to, considering we have museums for every other kind of space thing we've created. And for cars. And for art. And for watches and pottery and replicas of the body cast in metal or carved from stone.

We pay good money to see these works of art and technology.

I decided to write this chapter because I've observed how many people suffer inside bodies that are struggling to function optimally, struggling to perform their basic duties, struggling to heal. Many people live inside a body that is failing its human. Or they live inside a body that manages to function even though it is treated with disdain and disrespect. Some people curse their bodies for the pains and the aches and the discomfort they feel. Some curse their bodies, instead of thanking them for functioning despite their efforts to poison and disrespect them every day! Many people fill their bodies with toxic chemical sludge that the human body was never, ever designed to deal with.

Most often when a body is ailing, it is not failing us, we are failing it. Thirteen-plus BILLION years in the making of this miraculous machine, and then we poison it and kick it and yell at it to work better. Well, humans, if that's what you're doing, then wake up! Seriously! I'm writing this chapter for you, because caring for your miraculous body, the most advanced biological and technological creation in the known universe is not particularly difficult. It is not complex. It does not require a manual or a doctorate. It can be summed up in one sentence: Made by nature, fed by nature. Period. We are made of the body of the Earth. Of her elements. We are roughly 60 percent water, mixed with a bunch of carbon and other elements that can all be found, yes, in nature.

Nature, glorious Nature. SHE created the body and also created the fuel we need to feed and regenerate it day after day. So if you want to follow the simplest diet in the whole world, follow this one: Only eat foods that come directly from the Earth and have little to no processing or molestation. A perfect example is the apple. (For the moment, please disregard the fact that humans are now genetically modifying this wonderful creation and the fact that many farmers spray apples with toxic chemicals.) I'm talking about a perfect, ripe, beyond organic (dare I say, *biodynamic*) apple. From nature, by nature, for nature. A simple apple contributes to our wellness in so many ways that it's considered by some to be a superfood. That might be the reason for the saying "An apple a day keeps the doctor away."

And folks, WE are nature. Get it? I hear so many silly humans talk about nature as if it were a scary beast or something "out there." Run to the nearest mirror and gaze at the beast! We are an animal among animals. Some say the ultimate animal, the top of the food chain. But we don't act like it.

We take nature's bounty, HER grains, HER animal flesh, HER fruits, HER nuts, HER leafy green goodness, and we render them unrecognizable through processing. Then we add artificial colors and flavors and preservatives, and God knows what else, so that they taste better (some say) and last longer on the shelf, and we call the result *food*.

Folks, if you think that's food, then I have some swampland to sell you in Florida. That isn't food. It is processed, bastardized, chemically synthesized, modified (genetically and otherwise) garbage that when left out and offered to the biological, natural world remains untouched and unwanted by even the most simple of organisms. And yet we call it food, attempt to fuel our spacesuits with it, and wonder why we ache and suffer and breakdown, or why diseases like diabetes and cancer have become so commonplace that we simply accept them regrettably, yet expectantly. It is as if we knew they would come eventually, but hoped we could avoid or escape them for just a bit longer.

Poor nutrition from making the choice to eat unwholesome food comes with the sentence of disease and death. We say "Why me?" and our family and friends and society feel sorry for us as they witness us, seemingly unfairly, sentenced to a horrific state of disease or death, but we're the ones responsible.

Just so we are clear, I'm not talking about true diseases that inflict the young upon birth or shortly thereafter (although some of those illnesses might be attributable to conditions of diet and lifestyle during gestation). And I'm not talking about genetic diseases that can afflict any of us anytime. Yes, there are some sicknesses that are truly gruesome and ugly and horrific and I do not minimize the suffering they bring and the pain they cause.

But look around, there are many diseases, including some kinds of cancer, Type 2 diabetes, and Alzheimer's disease (which some people are now calling Type 3 diabetes) that without question are connected to poor eating habits and self-inflicted toxicity.

Poor habits are what I'm speaking to in this chapter. If you smoke, eat fast food, or your idea of a grocery store is the local convenience store, then stop complaining when your biology fails you because it is a predictable problem. If when you check out at the grocery store, the bulk of what you are taking home with you with will be microwaved or shoved into an oven preheated to 350 degrees, I'm talking to you! Does your body ache, do you have trouble sleeping, thinking, performing basic daily functions, such as digesting, pooping, having sex? Then walk to the mirror and say to yourself, "Shame on me for my afflictions." Own it. You did this to you! You failed your body. It did not fail you.

Who doesn't like junk food? It's literally designed for us to become addicted to it and crave it. Who doesn't like candy and soda and chicken nuggets and Cheetos®, or a McDonald's® Happy Meal® with a TOY IN IT? Even I admit to the fact that when I was a boy and my dear, sweet momma, who took such care to feed us wholesome, healthy, unprocessed food, asked me what I wanted for my birthday dinner (each year she would literally make us kids anything we wanted—lamb, filet mignon, lobster . . . anything—on our birthdays), my response one year was, "Swanson® TV dinner, Salisbury Steak." I kid you not. I just didn't understand why we had to eat brown rice and vegetables, and why sugary sodas and cereals were banned from our cupboards, while my friends down the way got to have Cap'n Crunch's cereal for breakfast and TV dinners for dinner. They were so good.

The neighbor kids' mother even called my mother alarmed because I did not know what a TV dinner was. My mother responded, "No, why would he? I've never bought a TV dinner for my kids." And these were our good friends with whom our family frequently vacationed—not much different from us.

My point here is that you have to choose to feed your biology and not your taste buds or your cravings. Like everything else in this book is about choice, what you put into your mouth is a choice. If your food choices are governed by cravings for garbage engineered to elicit addictive cravings, then your biology will eventually revolt, it will suffer, you will suffer, and disease will be the ultimate result. It is that simple.

Like every other biological being on this planet, our bodies function on a basic principle of fuel in, waste out. Every day, in addition to the trillions of other functions our bodies perform, they work diligently to deliver nature's elemental building blocks to our cells, tissues, and organs, so that they can function, heal, regenerate, replicate, and serve the greater purpose that is US. They do so tirelessly, unrelentingly, and with precision day in and day out, month in and month out, year in and year out. It is a full-time job every day to digest and metabolize our food and then "take out the trash" and eliminate the waste byproduct from our biological systems through the skin, the urinary tract, and the bowels (*ugh,* that word makes me shudder).

Our organs of elimination have full-time jobs taking out the trash so that our biological systems can function optimally. And that's if we feed our bodies pure, natural (as in directly from nature), unmolested, unprocessed fuel. Literally, theirs is a FULL-TIME, CEASELESS job to "take out the trash" in order to maintain balance and homeostasis. This process requires lots of fresh, living water and movement to be performed. Yet we pour the polluted, chlorinated, fluoridated liquid we call *water* into our biology and then sit on our butts on a couch or at a desk all day long and expect our miraculous bodies to work extra hard to compensate, to literally push the garbage uphill, in the snow, barefoot, both ways to/from school, in a hurricane of disrespect—and we complain when we have aches and pains.

Do you know about your lymphatic system? Not many people do. The lymphatic system is a network of tissues and organs that help rid the body of toxins, waste, and other unwanted materials. Did you know we have twice as much lymph in our bodies as blood or that we have twice as many lymph vessels as blood vessels? Did you also know that there is no equivalent to the heart to move this mass of fluid so that the required elimination of waste and fighting of infections can be achieved?

So, you might ask, what moves this mass of fluid? What is the engine that allows this mysterious, yet significant system to function? Well, folks, I will tell you. Movement. The body in motion is what allows the lymphatic system to function. Many of our lymph nodes are located in the groin area and under the arms. It is no coincidence that the simple act of walking involves the natural motion of swinging opposite arm with opposite leg, because as we walk, as we resist and succumb to gravity, as our muscles work and as we breathe in and out lymph is pumped through our body.

Why is the operation of this critical system not more common knowledge? Why doesn't every doctor explain how this works to us? Why aren't we taught this in physical education class during grade school? Everyone focuses on the cardiovascular system and NO ONE tells anyone anything about this other, larger, and equally critical system.

Movement and exercise is not just for the heart, but for the whole body. Movement is required to maintain health and homeostasis, and yet we spend most of our days sitting and preventing the body, the vehicle we were gifted for our earthly adventures, from doing what it is so perfectly and beautifully designed to do: fuel our cells with energy and nutrients and eliminate toxins, the byproduct of our biological processes. Without movement, those toxins build up. If we are not getting enough exercise, then daily we pour in more toxins from food and air and water and the toxins build up in our bodies. Day after day, month after month, and year after year. Considering that we're not moving, why do we ask, "WHY me cancer?" or WHY me diabetes? WHY have you chosen me?"

If we are to be radically honest with ourselves, we have to admit that we choose to ignore the needs of our bodies. We choose good health by eating wholesome food, drinking fresh water, and exercising. We choose poor health by choosing to consume one Twinkie®, one Slim Jim®, one McDonald's® Happy Meal®, one Swanson® TV dinner, one soda pop, one Pepperidge Farm® Goldfish® at a time. We choose it one bite or gulp at a time.

The second principle of maintaining our brilliant, vibrant biology besides feeding it only the fuel of nature, by nature, and for nature, unmolested and minimally processed, is that garbage in leads to garbage out. The more days or weeks or months where garbage in is greater than garbage out, the more likely it is that we are providing the perfect comfy home for the very diseases we so fervently pray to avoid.

But hope is not lost, my beautiful humans. Hope is never lost. Because this moment, right now, is a new moment. It is pregnant with new possibilities and new choices and new realities and new paths longing for you to discover them. So stop reading at the end of this chapter and find the nearest full-length mirror to look into. If this activity requires you to stand on the edge of your tub, then do so . . . carefully. I want you to strip down naked and then look at your spacesuit in the mirror, and I want you to love it with all your heart. Love it for its service. Love it for the miracle that it is. Love it for loving you despite the abuses it has suffered at your hands. Love it as it loves you: without judgment. Tell it you love it. Touch it, run your hands through its hair, over its skin, over your eyes. All of it is miraculous. You are observing and admiring and appreciating OUR most magnificent creation.

Own your body in whatever state you observe it, and now that you understand a bit more about how to care for it, make a promise to it (and yourself) that you will choose better. Promise to go forth and learn how to better care for it. Promise you will seek knowledge and guidance in whatever form is appropriate to help you choose better. Then do so.

We can choose thoughts, words, and actions instead of allowing our patterns and programs to choose them for us. This means that you can choose to put pure natural food into your mouth instead of letting your cravings for unhealthy foods choose for you. Choose! If you haven't gotten this message yet, then I don't know what to tell you. You always have a choice, ALWAYS.

When you stare at the menu in a restaurant or walk down the aisles of your grocery store, you have a choice. Choose wisely.

The reason why there is hope is that the body is innately driven to heal and seeks tirelessly to return you, and itself, to a state of health and equilibrium. The moment you choose to feed it pure food and pure water, and to breathe pure air, the healing begins. Depending on your state of toxicity/imbalance, you might temporarily feel worse before you feel better, but you WILL FEEL BETTER! Commit. Choose health, and you will heal. The aches and pains will subside, you will need less of the medications you rely on, and in some cases you will be able to cease taking them altogether. Stay committed and you will witness the powerful miracle of regeneration and healing. It is miraculous. *(Caution: Stopping taking medication on your own may be hazardous. Always seek the guidance of a healthcare professional before tapering off.)*

I am forty-eight years old as I write this and I experience no aches and pains. None. There is nothing I cannot do physically. Now there are things I *will not* do because I just don't want to, but I am not limited in any way by my biology. My body and I have a wonderful relationship. I have learned to listen to it. It, like the Universe, speaks to me every day, telling me what it needs to function optimally.

"More water please. No, not that water. Yes, *that* water."

"More movement please."

"Bone broth, please. And fermented raw sauerkraut for my digestion, please."

I listen and I learn and I seek to know better how to love and feed my body, and the whole process is fun and I feel fantastic. I get to move about, exploring MY creation in a body that happily obeys my commands for thought and movement. Glorious! I invite you to experience this reality for yourself.

Although it might seem for some that this reality exists only at the end of a long, exhausting, arduous journey that feels like the equivalent of climbing Mount Everest without a Sherpa or oxygen, you CAN do it—just don't look at the top of the mountain and scare yourself. Look down at your feet (those awesome, complex feet with more bones than any other part of your body) and simply take one step. Then another. Find others who are on a similar journey and take a step with them.

There are millions of us out there. In fact there are more of us every day awakening to the power we have to heal our bodies. Join together with a friend and support each other. You cannot and should not do this alone. Just keep putting one beautiful foot in front of another.

And if you stumble or fall, or even if you seemingly go crashing ass over teakettle down a steep incline to the bottom of the gorge as a result of a weeklong binge on soda, Ho Hos®, and pork rinds, simply pick yourself up, dust yourself off, laugh at your silliness, forgive yourself fully, and step again. It will get easier, I promise, and the reward will be experiencing the vibrant health that is your birthright.

While I am meticulous about my diet and 99 percent of the time impeccable about what I put into and on my body, I am also a human playing in my creation, and I love me some banana cream pie, fried chicken, or chicken-fried steak with mashed potatoes! We humans have created some scrumptious treats, have we not? I mean, a gooey-centered chocolate cake? Come on! Triple crème cheese? Bacon? Or one of my all-time favorites, Chubby Hubby® ice cream from Ben & Jerrys? And I rarely stop at a few bites and usually find myself scraping the bottom of the pint longing for MORE.

I'm not a monk. I have desires beyond "being good and conscious" all the time. But even in moments when I choose to eat what I KNOW does not optimally feed my biology (and might even result in a crippling food coma), I say to my body, "Body, I'm good to you, so you just hush, 'cause I want me some ooey-goo-ey, crunchy, salty, sweet deliciousness and I'm gonna have it."

And do you know what? It has no objection—well, except for the food coma or resulting headache or diarrhea. But dammit, it's worth it.

I could give you more info here about how and what to eat. I could share my personal philosophy about food, types of food, and how to prepare different foods. I could even share info about the supplements I have tirelessly researched and take every day. But there are volumes already written on these matters and I think everyone must find their own dietary truth depending on what resonates with them. I am not for or against any particular approach. I would suggest only that you not take anyone's opinion without testing things out and seeing how you feel. Your body will always tell you.

CHAPTER NINETEEN

COME HOME TO YOU

*The Earth is populated with more than
seven billion messiahs who have come forth
to remember, awaken, and come home
to the knowing of I AM.*

Ultimately, any resistance to our own becoming is futile. Just as a caterpillar cannot resist becoming a butterfly and an acorn cannot resist becoming a mighty oak tree, the two cells that come together to create a human cannot help striving to fulfill their potential. Becoming is the nature of the Universe—and of human nature.

Now, as you observe your outer world, you might be thinking that you are not realizing your potential or that some of your fellow humans are not achieving their potentials. To this, I say not every potential is a great one. Not every potential looks like our culture's version of success and fulfillment, such as earning buckets of money or academic degrees, becoming president, running a multibillion-dollar corporation, playing professional sports, or being a popstar or famous actor—although it could look like those things and for some it does.

Remember, in every moment we are potentialized simply because we are! This moment could be no other way than it is given everything that has happened in our lives to this point. All the forces of the Universe and our own divine free will have converged here and now to make it so.

This does not mean that everyone will reach his or her ultimate potential. Just as every acorn does not become a mighty oak—some lay on the ground and rot, becoming food for insects and topsoil or are eaten by squirrels—so too do many humans reach a particular potential in themselves and stop consciously participating or creating. The wondrous Universe does not love them any less for this. SHE celebrates their choices regarding who and what they choose to become. SHE equally celebrates a great artist or a mighty politician or a CEO or a monk or a lama or a guru or a bank teller or a refuge manager or a home-less child or a criminal. To the Universe, there are no levels of success and there is no success, there is only what is. There is only being and becoming.

Wherever you end up, there you are. How glorious!

One of my favorite lines from Abraham-Hicks goes something like: "You can't get it wrong and you will never get it done." This is the simplest and truest of truths. Whatever you accomplish or do with your life, it cannot be wrong, because the Grand Universe that created All That Is, Was, and Will Be does not get it wrong, EVER! And as long as you draw breath, you are not done because you are always changing, always participating—consciously and unconsciously—in the dance of creation in small and large ways.

When I meet people who have ceased to question or actively grow or seek, those who have given in to the current conditions of their lives, I imagine that the gravitational pull of all the wounds and experiences and pains they've endured in their lives is so strong that they cannot achieve escape velocity from them. Like rockets that cannot break free of the Earth's atmosphere, they are stuck orbiting within the stories of their suffering.

But that's OK, for eventually, like the rest of us, they will return home just as drops of water return to the ocean—rain-ing, snowing, dripping into the streams that lead to the rivers that feed the whole. They are equally as welcomed as anyone else is—welcomed without judgment—on the beautiful Planet Earth in the region of space we humans call the Milky Way Gal-axy. They are celebrated by the Universe for their courage to do the dance of matter and Spirit as an individual fragment of the whole with opportunities to awaken, to become, to remem-ber, to rise. No creature, plant, idea, human, organization, or planet is brought forth into this material reality without having the knowing and wisdom to guide its own becoming and push itself toward the greatest, most divine expression of itself incrementally over its lifespan.

It's easy to slip into the habit of judging ourselves for how we've potentialized. Of all the aspects of my character that I've worked on, I've worked hardest on letting go of judgment—perhaps the most dangerous and harmful of human acts. It, along with forgiveness, has been challenging for me. But when I lived in a cabin in the woods for five years in the Hudson Valley of New York State, I learned nonjudgment from nature. I watched the trees and the bears and the squirrels and the hawks, and my chickens and the snakes and the insects, and I learned that judgment does not exist on Earth except in the minds of humans. Judgment is a human creation. Nor do forgiveness or the lack thereof, which are both related to the process of judging an act or behavior as "bad." In nature there is never judgment or anything to forgive. There is only cause and effect, action/reaction, hunter/hunted, gentleness and violence, rain and sunshine, wind and stillness, warmth and cold.

I raised chickens that were killed by hawks in violent and bloody attacks, and life went on. I saw baby chicks die at the beaks of others in the flock, and life went on, with the hens continuing to live together peacefully. I saw nature benevolently allowing her creatures to fully be what they were designed to be—and sometimes this involved violence and killing and death. Sometimes this involved beauty and harmony. Sometimes it didn't. Hawks feed on chickens and other smaller birds and tiny creatures. It's necessary for their survival to hunt. It's part of how this perfectly divine ecosystem functions. Everything is food for something else.

No state of being or becoming is preferred over the other or judged to be better or worse, good or bad by chickens, hawks, or the Universe. Only we think like that.

We humans judge. But if we are to be free, individually and collectively, we must cease this action! It is judgment of self by others (and by the self that has been programmed by others) that keeps us small and inhibits our becoming fully potentialized.

You're doing no one any favors by impeding your own becoming. You will give yourself, humanity, the Earth, and all the rest of creation the biggest gift you can if you GIVE THEM THE GIFT OF YOU: all of you, the best of you, the YOU that you were born to be. Give it without apology or judgment. If you do, then all of creation will celebrate.

I celebrate you fully for being fully YOU! I'll even get out my pom-poms and cheer for you loudly and embarrassingly! Then I will call you over, saying, "*PSSST,* come here," and tell you what the Universe told me once I gave my whole self fully to HER and told HER I would do HER bidding on this planet. She embraced me and said, "You are not alone my child, but one of many. You are part of an organism that lives on the body of the Earth called human. Now that you have come home to YOU, you must help others come home to THEMSELVES. You must love them as I do, no matter what.

"You must show the cruel kindness.

"You must show the weak strength.

"You must show the sad joy.

"And you must help them rise!

"Call it enlightened self-interest if that makes you feel better. None of you can come home to the collective YOU of humanity until all the pieces of that collective are gathered together into WE. While one human suffers, your work is not done.

"But remember, I do not ask you to save anyone or do anything—not even to save the Earth. I am not putting a heavy burden on your shoulders. I am simply asking that you go out into the world and shine your light. Support and guide others when called upon to do so. Sing your singular note and dance your unique dance, and show others, by your example, what it looks like to come home to the YOU I created you to be and express itself in MY creation."

Hearing this, I cried and cried and cried. Could it be so simple? Could this be all that the Universe wants from us? Why do we struggle so? We silly, silly humans.

I have spent thirty years searching for my joy. Searching for an end to the pain and suffering of living. Searching for the ME I was born to be. I've been trying to return to the beautiful, innocent, powerful boy I was before the experiences of life obscured my brilliance with layer after layer of black goo. It's been a long, hard journey on which I can't count the number of times that I thought to myself, *"I'm done. I just can't take another step."* But I did take the next step. And then I took another and another, until I arrived here and now I am writing these words.

The journey started with my nineteen-year-old self who quit college in his third trimester and cried every day. I was broken and unhappy to a degree I couldn't tolerate and I didn't know what to do. I had no tools to understand why I was miserable or to look for the root causes of my deep suffering. The pain was constant and unrelenting. I didn't know how to stop it.

I wasn't one to turn to alcohol or drugs for relief, so I just sat in it and suffered until I realized I could end the pain. I did have that choice. I could end my life and the pain would stop. So I sat with this choice. I don't remember if it was days or weeks that I sat with it, but I did. I pondered it and sunk into the power I had to end my suffering. I stewed in it and let it soak into me. I had the ultimate choice to be or to not be, and I chose to be. Obviously. But I didn't just choose to be and to continue suffering. I resolved to figure it out, to search for truth and to root out the cause of my suffering. I decided I would not stop until I found the key to a happier life because I CHOSE to live. Living didn't choose me.

I certainly wasn't going to live another sixty, seventy, or eighty years in the reality I was experiencing. I couldn't. If I didn't find the answers I was seeking it would be like slowly burning to death over an eighty-year span and I wasn't willing to endure that kind of constant, inexhaustible pain.

That's why I went to my mother and said I need to leave and go somewhere and be by myself. I need to get away and just be. I need to experience who I am, what I am, and why I am. I booked a trip to the Yucatan Peninsula in Mexico and packed a backpack. Before then, I was not one to be alone; I was always with friends or family. I couldn't (OK, I wouldn't) eat alone in public and I didn't yet do things by myself, so this in itself was a huge step for me.

I bought the ticket and just set out on my journey. First stop, Cozumel, an island off the coast of Cancun. I don't think I even had a hotel room when I arrived, but I found one in town. Before I left I had grabbed some books from my mom's "woo-woo" library. It was endlessly embarrassing to my nineteen-year-old self who cared so much what others thought and had worked so hard to fit in to have a mother who had placed crystals all over our house and read all these weird books. But as I look back at her choices I am filled with enormous gratitude because it's clear to me that she prepared the fertile soil for my awakening. I grabbed three books that "spoke" to me: *Jonathan Livingston Seagull* by Richard Bach, *The Road Less Traveled* by M. Scott Peck, and *Illusions* by Richard Bach. These books spoke to me in ways that I can't begin to convey precisely, except to say that they ignited a spark of knowing and remembering deep within me that would become the fire that drove me forward.

When I prepared for my trip, I didn't know to prepare for what it felt like to be alone. I was learning how to be just me. Not me trying to be a version of me that I thought others would like or approve of. Not me anticipating and trying to avoid the pain of criticism and judgment by my horribly judgmental peers who were each only doing the best they could. Man, oh man, can kids be mean. Me included. *OUCH.* All the time. *Ouch!* So there I was, just me with me being me. And for the first time since I was six or seven, I felt relief. I felt free. No one was watching me. No one had an opinion about me or my behavior or my choices. Even the thinking mind in me that had been programmed by all these external forces for a reason that's still unknown to me decided it would take a vacation from me at the very time I was taking a vacation for ME, so I was also relieved even of self-judgment.

And guess what, the crying stopped. The suffering stopped. The heaviness lifted. The clouds parted and a smile returned to my boyish, sweet face! The goodness that I remembered emanating from the young boy I had been before life came crashing in returned. And that was the most powerful experience of all. I remembered who I was and I got to touch a part of myself that I had buried deep and away. Away from the world that hurt me.

Away from a world that didn't deserve me.

Of course, in locking ME away from the world and people I had locked ME away from myself. Because of this I suffered. Oh, how I had suffered! But the suffering ended as soon as I came home to ME.

This was my first homecoming. Down in Mexico, we played and played and played, me and ME, me of nineteen with me of seven. We laughed and we danced and we were silly. And we voraciously devoured the books I had brought with me and they helped me remember, especially *Jonathan Livingston Seagull* and *Illusions,* that to be different is beautiful, even when it hurts. Also that within us is all the magic and power of the Universe and we are each capable of great things.

When I was a boy, our elderly babysitter Mildred used to take me and my siblings to Sunday school. I must have been six or seven. And I remember sitting there and listening to the teachings and saying, "Wait, you've got this all wrong, don't you see?" God didn't want us to worship him. He wanted to tell us that we are him and he is us. God is our potential realized. At seven I was confident that I was a messiah. That I was special. That we are all special.

Down in Mexico, I got to come home to this knowing and to myself, and it was only the start of the journey I've been on ever since. It has been a long, hard, fun, exhausting, exhilarating, and excruciating journey. I truly cannot believe that I am here, now, writing these words and experiencing another more permanent homecoming. Because you see, even though I came home to me when I was nineteen, I could not hold on to the experience of being awakened or remain there, so I woke and slept, and woke and slept, and I have crashed my creation bus often from then to now, mowing down many an innocent soul in the process (not literally, of course).

Finally, I stopped taking steps on my path, took a look around, and decided I was done searching. If I hadn't found whatever it was I was looking for in thirty years of searching, then maybe it wasn't possible to find it. If I hadn't found it in the zillions of books I read, seminars I took, and retreats I traveled far and wide to attend, then maybe there was no end to this journey. I was tired. Tired of hoping and wanting and searching. Deeply tired. So I sat down and gave up the search. It's kind of like the moment in the film *Forest Gump* when Forest decides to stop running. He is just done. So he goes home.

I stopped and decided that instead of searching I would start doing. And I said to the Universe, "OK, enough of the searching. I don't even care if I find whatever it was that I was looking for anymore. I just want to be done with the searching."

And the Universe said, "Good, let's get to work."

After that, I moved from searching to doing, and daily asked the Universe, "What is it that you want me to do today?" Sometimes the answer was as simple as giving someone a smile, and other times I actually had to stop and give more of myself and my insights to a person or a company that needed guidance. Sometimes I got paid and sometimes I didn't. But I found I always had enough. Actually, I always had *more than enough.* When I got scared that I wouldn't have enough, money always came just when I needed it. Like magic.

Then one day, I was hanging out with a friend in Madison, Wisconsin, my dear, sweet, wonderful brother Matty D. We were talking about the end of the searching and the darkness that preceded the end of my searching, and I had an insight. "You know what?" I told Matt, "I just realized that when I stopped searching, I actually found what I was looking for: ME. I spent thirty years and God only knows how much time and money and energy searching and suffering, and all the while here I was, just waiting for myself to come home. Just waiting to stop searching and realize that the ME the Universe designed ME to be never left me. It was always with me and within me. It was I who left me. And now I am home."

I look around and see a world of people struggling and searching and banging around on the planet trying to figure "IT" out. The energy and time and resources we spend collectively on this process are staggering. We are all striving and doing our best in any given moment. I know I've "failed" (if there is such a thing) and I've fallen, HARD. I've hurt others and been hurt. I've suffered and caused suffering. I've loved and been loved. I've hated and been hated. Because I've done all these things and been all these things, I cannot judge anyone else for doing or being them. It is simply not fair or right to do so. Nor would it be fair to judge degrees of these things, considering that degrees ranging from zero to infinity are simply other states of a thing's being. Other versions of how it can be potentialized.

Like me, you are simply trying to come home to yourself. And like I discovered on my trip to the Yucatan thirty years ago, the thing that most stands in your way is the judgment of others (real or perceived) and your judgment of yourself.

Let us stop judging ourselves and each other, and instead use the energy we formerly spent on judgment and struggle to uplift each other. Let us expend it on being kind to each other and helping each other to rise into our greatness, becoming the most remarkable expressions of creation we can become. Let us spend our energy on coming home to ourselves and helping others come home to themselves. Let's come home to the knowing we are beings of stardust dancing within a 3D sliver of an infinite reality.

Fellow humans, it's time to wake up! Time to stop searching and struggling and to start doing and being. RIGHT NOW. It's time to stop wanting and start creating. To stop trying and start making shit happen. Full on. No limits.

The Universe needs and wants only one thing: for each of us to sing our singular note into the symphony of creation. Sing it loudly. Sing it proudly. And sing like it matters—like you matter! Because while we are specks of dust living on a speck of dust in an infinite Universe, we are also particles of GOD, we are significantly insignificant, insignificantly significant, and perfectly imperfect.

Today I look at the Earth and I see that it is populated with more than SEVEN BILLION messiahs who have come forth to remember, to awaken, and come home to the knowing of I AM: I am unique. I am magnificent. I am enough. I am beautiful. I am perfect just as I am. Because I AM the Universe, and SHE doesn't make any mistakes! We are here to awaken to this truth together.

All of us. Muslim and Jew. Black and white. Old and young. Rich and poor. Skinny and fat. Weak and strong. Artist and banker. Politician and teacher. Being part of the Universe is like being one of the Three Musketeers: All for one and one for all. And as the Universe told me, we've got work to do, because none of us is truly awakened until all of us are awakened. Fortunately, we only need to choose it!

All that's needed is to choose to think and speak and act as the Universe enshrouded in matter. Live that reality as an example for others, so they can choose it too. And if others need your support and guidance to know and remember, help them. Offer your hand, your heart, an ear to listen, and uplift them by seeing them in all their perfection.

ACKNOWLEDGEMENTS

acknowledge myself for being brave enough to question, struggle, live, learn, hurt, love, cry, sweat, laugh, forgive, succeed, fail, and become. I thank the Earth for my wonderful, miraculous human body and the Creator/Universe for the spark of her that lives within me and shines and sings through me as me.

I also would like to acknowledge all my guides and teachers on the journey, especially those who have been with me longest: my family. Thanks to my mother, Susie; my brother, Brian; my sister, Dinah; and my father, Tom, who left too soon to see the man I've become. I am also grateful for the family I am fortunate to have gathered along the way, my family of choice: my friends. Friends have held me, loved me, carried me, and allowed me to love and carry them through the struggles and the ease of life. Thank you, Scott Watkins, Darrel Wilson, Russ Pangborn, Brett Toston, Shari Dunbar/Boyer, Karen McDowell/Brown, Tim Howard, Tippy Bushkin, Tom Sloan, Brad Lande, Ian Richer, Theo Souliopoulos, Matt D'Amour, Starlight D'Amour, Christine Prebil, Jim Prebil, Amber Rubarth, Diane Buckalew, Jim Buckalew, Dorothy Porter, Greg Vogel, Todd Giorgi, Derek D'Alessandro, Doug Hetrick, Ken Colgan, and many, many others. I have not done it alone, and there are no words for the depth and breadth of love and support you have given me. I am here because of you, able to write this book because of you.

A very special acknowledgement to my friend Rebecca Ryan who read an early version of this book when it was maybe eight chapters and only 20,000-words long, who said, "YES, this is amazing. Keep going, please keep going." The Universe spoke through her just when I needed the encouragement to emancipate myself from doubt.

Another very special acknowledgement to my editor, Stephanie Gunning, who helped me turn nineteen disorganized chapters and 45,000 words into 63,000-plus words that I am proud to call *Potentialized* on this day, Valentine's Day, February 14, 2016.

Another very special acknowledgement to Zac Shaw, who

helped me market and design the book, and more important-ly, whose belief and enthusiasm for the book and its message pulled me back into the flow and excitement of the process more than once.

Finally, to those of you who have picked up this book and read it through to these words, thank you for giving this message life. Thank you for finding your way to it and allowing it in! It is my sincere hope that your road ahead has been made easier and that the unique spark I know you are can dance and shine a little brighter for having had the experience of reading this book.

ABOUT THE AUTHOR

Bradley Thomason is a human. An adventurer. A seeker. A student. A teacher. A brother. A son. A friend. And now apparently, an author. He has dedicated his life to seeking and learning and becoming and remembering. His career has seen him as a student, an investment banking analyst, an actor, a salesman, a marketer, a waiter, a nothing, a VP, a Chief Visionary Officer, a founder, an entrepreneur, a failure, and a success. He has not yet gotten it right—although not for lack of trying. And he is not yet done, because his heart still beats and he still draws breath. He vowed years ago to serve the force that created him by working with individual humans, their ideas, and/or their organizations to help realize their unique and powerful potential. To this end, he formed Potentialized LLC. Lastly, he is a potentialized, potentializing potentializer.

Bradley lives wherever he is called to do his work and is always accompanied by his dog and unwavering friend, Max (formerly Kodi, formerly Brooks).

Visit Bradley at:

▸ Website: Potentialized.com
▸ Twitter: @URpotentialized
▸ Facebook: facebook.com/potentialized

Made in the USA
Columbia, SC
18 April 2017